PERSON TO PERSON:

The Orthodox Understanding
of Human Nature

PERSON TO PERSON

The Orthodox Understanding of Human Nature

HARRY BOOSALIS

ST. TIKHON'S MONASTERY PRESS
SOUTH CANAAN, PENNSYLVANIA 18459
2018

PERSON TO PERSON:
The Orthodox Understanding of Human Nature

The Holy Icon of Glykophilousa (detail) is from
the Holy Monastery of Philotheou, Mount Athos,
used with kind permission.

Published by:
St. Tikhon's Monastery Press
175 St. Tikhon's Road
Waymart, Pennsylvania 18472
USA

Printed in the United States of America

ISBN – 978-1-7328522-0-4

For

Archimandrite Nathaniel

and the Brotherhood
of the Holy Monastery of Iveron

TABLE OF CONTENTS

CHAPTER THREE: PANAYIA

CHAPTER FOUR: IN THE IMAGE AND LIKENESS OF GOD

ABOUT THE AUTHOR

Dr. Harry Boosalis, Th. D., graduated from Holy Cross Greek Orthodox School of Theology (Master of Divinity degree, Class of 1985) and received his doctoral degree in Orthodox Theology from the University of Thessalonica under the direction of Professor Georgios Mantzaridis. He has been teaching Dogmatic Theology at St. Tikhon's Orthodox Seminary since the Fall of 1992. His other books include *Orthodox Spiritual Life*, *The Joy of the Holy*, *Knowledge of God*, *Taught by God*, *Holy Tradition* and *Angels and Demons*, all published by St. Tikhon's Monastery Press.

PREFACE

Contemporary western society questions what it means to be human. Competing and contradictory ideologies argue over the purpose of life, gender, sexual orientation and personal identity. Anthropological confusion could characterize our generation.

The Orthodox understanding of human nature is unique. It differs from every philosophy, religion and Christian denomination. This book presents a clear and concise introduction to the Orthodox understanding of what it means to be human.

Topics such as the relationship between our soul and body, the profound significance of human freedom, the meaning of our creation in the image and likeness of God, and the person of Panayia, are all examined in light of Orthodox Tradition.

Grounded in Holy Scripture and patristic teachings, this study refers to writings from a variety of contemporary Orthodox Saints, Elders and theologians. Although written for seminarians preparing for the Holy Priesthood, the language and style will appeal to lay readers as well.

Amid the ever-changing and divergent views of what it means to be human, the teaching of the Orthodox Church remains especially relevant, and liberating, for today.

Chapter One: The Human Body

"God sanctifies also the very members of our bodies."

St. Maximos the Confessor

Preliminary Points

Contemporary man is obsessed with his body. This pertains not only to his own body, but to the bodies of others as well. We scrutinize each other's body.

We're into body-building and body-piercing. We tan our body and tattoo our body. We try to enhance our body through plastic surgery. We even surgically alter the gender of our body, in order to match our sexual orientation.

Much of this is a manifestation of our materialistic and carnal-minded culture. But if we look deeper, perhaps this reveals a fundamental flaw in how we see ourselves and how we see each other.

Upon closer observation, a tendency toward two extremes is apparent. On one hand, we take great effort to pamper and indulge our bodies. The advertising industry exploits and encourages sensuality. Seductive images of the human body are plastered throughout the Internet, in magazines and on gigantic billboards, enticing us with various products. There is an over-infatuation with the body. For many, the human body has become an idol.

13

On the other hand, our society openly disparages the human body. We discard the body through abortion, before it is born, and dispose the body through cremation once it dies.

We give little thought to the natural and organic relationship between our soul and body. For many people, the common belief is that a human being is basically composed of an immaterial soul (or 'consciousness') which is *temporarily* embedded in a material container, the body. According to this belief, this union is not permanent.

Some religions teach that our soul may be re-incarnated into another body. And when that body dies, our soul continues to be re-incarnated, until attaining the ultimate spiritual state—that of no longer having a body at all.

Other philosophies teach that our soul was never meant to inhabit a body in the first place. According to this teaching, our soul existed *before* the body—our soul 'pre-existed' in a bodiless state. For this school of thought, as a result of a primeval fall, our soul is now trapped within our body and longs to be released from its prison. Here again, the highest form of human existence is for the soul to be freed from the shackles of the body, so it may return to the bodiless state from which it originated.

The Orthodox Church teaches differently. Our soul is not meant to exist *apart* from our body, nor our body apart from the soul. There is an innate and everlasting unity between our soul and body. They will forever be united as one.

"The soul possesses such a natural union of love with its particular body that it never wants to abandon it,"[1] writes St. Gregory Palamas. Our body and soul are intended to function together in a harmonious and reciprocal relationship as one.[2]

According to Orthodox teaching, both our body and soul *together* make up our human person: "Every body is connected with one soul, and every soul is connected with one body, and the two together constitute the particular [person], a definite man."[3] Our soul was not created to be separated from our body.

Sin and Death

There is one exception of course—during that un-natural and temporary tragedy of death. Death is one of life's great mysteries. Our understanding of death reflects our understanding of life. How we see death impacts how we see ourselves, the world around us, and God.

---

[1] St. Gregory Palamas, *Natural Chapters* 38, PG 150, 1148A, trans. Palmer, Sherrard and Ware, *The Philokalia* 4, London, 1995, p. 363. See St. Gregory of Nyssa, *On the Making of Man* 29, PG 44, 233D and St. Epiphanios of Salamis, *Panarion* 64. 18, PG 41, 1097D.

[2] "For the Bible ... the terms 'body' and 'soul' are not essentially constituent parts, but two different ways of seeing man as a whole ... For Biblical man, a human being is a personalized unity." Hierom. Makarios of Simonopetra, *The Greek, Hebrew and Christian Perceptions of the Body*, in *Synaxis* vol. 1, Montreal, 2006, p. 71.

[3] Metro. Hierotheos, *Life After Death*, trans. E. Williams, Levadia, 1996, p. 87.

Death is a fact of life. Yet the way we die is not as important as the way we approach it: "Will the death we are fac-
ing be transformed into a gift, a source of life, or will it
destroy us? This depends entirely on our attitude."[4]

Death is the direct outcome of sin. And sin is willful self-
separation from God: "But on as many as, according to
their own choice, depart from God, He inflicts that separation from Himself which they have chosen of their own
accord. But separation from God is death, and separation
from light is darkness."[5] Sin is when we separate ourselves from God.[6]

In Orthodoxy, sin is not viewed in a legalistic sense, such
as the breaking of a rule or regulation. Rather, sin is a spiritual sickness separating us from God, from each other
and from our true selves.

Sin is when we abuse our God-given freedom. We sin
when we make wrong choices that lead to our separation
from God's will and likeness.

---

[4] Arch. Zacharias, *Remember Thy First Love*, Waymart, 2016, p. 162.
Death is "the enemy to be destroyed, and not a mystery to be ex-
plained." Schmemann, *For the Life of the World*, Crestwood, 1973, p.
100.
[5] St. Irenaeus, *Against Heresies* 5. 27. 2, trans. Roberts and Donaldson (ANF, vol. 1), Peabody, 2004, p. 556.
[6] "A man knows God, and is known by Him, in so far as he makes
every effort not to be separated from God." St. Anthony the Great, *On
the Character of Men* 164, trans. *The Philokalia* 1, London, 1979, p. 354.

Sin prevents us from participating in divine life, leading ultimately to death: "For, behold, those who keep themselves far away from You shall perish."[7]

Death, for the Orthodox Church, is not a punishment for sin. God did not create death. He does not want it. What God wants is our freedom, even if this means we might choose living for and loving ourselves more than Him. God respects our freedom so much that He even allows us to separate ourselves from Him. Death is not a punishment so much as it is a natural outcome of what happens when we sin, when we cut ourselves off from the Source of true Life—God.

The idea that death is a punishment from God for breaking His commandments is based on an inaccurate interpretation of Genesis 2.16-17: "And the Lord God commanded the man, saying, 'Of every tree of the garden you may freely eat; but of the tree of the knowledge of good and evil you shall not eat, for in the day that you eat of it you shall surely die'."[8]

This does not say, 'If you eat of this particular tree, I will punish you with death'. Rather, from an Orthodox perspective, when God forewarned Adam, 'For in the day that you eat of it you shall surely die', He was clearly cautioning him that if he ate from this specific tree, he would be separating himself from the true life that God had given him.

---

[7] Psalms 72. 27 (SAAS).
[8] Gen 2. 16-17. (All Scriptural references are from the New King James Version, unless otherwise noted).

Far from what was originally intended by our Creator, the world is now bound by disease, dysfunction, destruction and death. This is not the world as originally created by God. It is the result of our misuse of our God-given freedom.

"*original sin*"

Our ensuing separation from God has led to dire consequences for the entire creation. Even though we are created in the image of God, in a world originally created good and beautiful, we are, in fact, born into a 'death-bound' universe: "All people taste the terrible mystery of death, since we all inherit corruptibility and mortality. In other words, we are born to die. Death is the surest, most certain event in our life."[9]

In many ways, however, we would rather forget death exists, seeking instead to preserve our youth. We lose sight of the fact that we have fallen from our original glory. This way of life—indeed this way of death—is not what God intends. Our separation from God results in death, engulfing the world since Adam's Fall.

2 forms of death

There are two kinds of death: *physical* death—the separation of our soul from our body; and *spiritual* death—the separation of our soul from God's grace: "Physical death is when the soul leaves the body and is separated from it. The death of the soul is when God leaves the soul and is separated from it ...

---

[9] Metro. Hierotheos, *Life After Death*, p. 22.

"Once separated from God the soul becomes more ugly and useless than a dead body, but unlike such a body it does not disintegrate after death ..."[10]

In spite of death, life is still good. Because of God's great benevolence, life on earth is indeed beautiful. Life is so beautiful that at times we consider our sinful condition, even death itself, as 'natural' to us—he 'died of *natural* causes'.

The truth is sin and death are *not* natural to us. Our willful separation from God's grace and the consequent separation of our soul from our body are indeed un-natural. Sin, sickness, senility; old age, death, and bodily corruption—all these are alien to our nature as human beings. God did not create us to suffer these things. These are all consequences of separating ourselves from God—in Whose image and likeness we are originally created: "I weep and I wail when I think upon death, and behold our beauty, fashioned after the image of God, lying in the tomb disfigured, dishonored, bereft of form."[11]

---

[10] St. Gregory Palamas, *Homilies* 16. 7, ed. and trans. C. Veniamin, Waymart, 2009, p. 118. See Met. Hierotheos, *Life After Death*, p. 22.
[11] *Funeral Hymn*, Tone 8 (St. John Damascene), *Service Book*, trans. I. Hapgood, Englewood, 1975, p. 386.

Garments of Skin

Holy Scripture describes man's fallen condition with the phrase 'garments of skin': "For Adam and his wife the Lord God made garments of skin, and clothed them."[12] 'Garments of skin' refers to our fallen, mortal state in which we now live, and will one day die.

Garments of skin are not equated with the human body *per se*, at least not as originally created by God. Rather, these 'garments' represent fallen man's new mortality which resulted from Adam's free choice to separate himself from God: "The central content of the 'garments of skin' is mortality, the transformation of life into survival. ... [God] tolerates within His infinite love even this new situation and transforms it into a blessing ... so that by using it correctly humanity can survive and realize its original goal in Christ."[13]

Prior to these garments of skin, pre-fallen Adam in Paradise was naked by virtue of his simplicity.[14] In other words, before the Fall, Adam lived in natural harmony with the world around him: "The body of Adam was so simple that it was in reality transparent, open to the material creation without resisting it in any way ..."[15]

---

[12] Gen. 3. 21.

[13] P. Nellas, *Deification in Christ*, trans. N. Russell, Crestwood, 1987, pp. 60-61.

[14] "He was naked because of his simplicity and life free from artifice and far from any covering ..." St. Gregory the Theologian, *Orations* 45. 8, PG 36, 632C, trans. N. Harrison, in *Festal Orations*, Crestwood, 2008, p. 167.

[15] P. Nellas, *Deification in Christ*, pp. 52-53.

When he fell, Adam broke his original relationship with God and the world. Our soul is now preoccupied—often obsessed—with passions of the flesh, worldly pleasures and material possessions. 'Garments of skin' conveys the reality that fallen man is now bound by a biological mode of existence. Man must now toil and sweat to sustain himself. He must protect himself against the elements—even from the animals originally created for him: "Man no longer has life in the way that he did previously ... Life continues only so long as death is postponed. That which exists now in the proper sense is death: 'life' has been transmuted into 'survival'."[16]

Bodily Death as a Benevolence of God

The Church Fathers teach that these 'garments of skin' reveal God's goodness and compassion for man. In light of God's great love and mercy, death is considered as a remedy for sin, not punishment. The inevitability of death can lead man to repentance and the struggle against sin.

St Basil the Great writes, "God did not create death, but we brought it upon ourselves by a wicked intention. ... He did not prevent our dissolution ... that our weakness might not remain as immortal."[17]

---

[16] P. Nellas, *Deification in Christ*, p. 47. See E. Theokritoff, "When Adam disobeyed the King above, the whole creation rose up against him ... The wild beasts turned hostile, the earth was unwilling to feed him ..." *Living in God's Creation*, Crestwood, 2009, p. 82.

[17] St. Basil, *God Is Not the Cause of Evil* 7, PG 31, 345AB, trans. N. Harrison, in *On the Human Condition*, Crestwood, 2005, p. 75.

St. Gregory the Theologian adds, "Yet here too [man] makes a gain, namely death and the cutting off of sin, in order that evil may not be immortal. Thus, his punishment is changed into a mercy..."[18] By tolerating death, God providentially limits the extent of man's sin and separation from Him.

Our mortality not only limits the extent of our sin, it also frees us from our personal sicknesses and sorrows. St. Cyril of Alexandria teaches: "By death the Giver of the Law stopped the spread of sin, and even in this He reveals His love for mankind. For death dissolves this animal nature of ours and stops the activity of evil, and on the other hand, it delivers or frees man from illnesses, frees him from labors, and puts an end to his sorrows and cares, and stops his bodily sufferings."[19]

In light of the Resurrected Christ, it is better for us to grow old and eventually die. This is to say, it is better that our soul be *temporarily* separated from our body, rather than allow our unnatural separation from God to last forever.

---

[18] St. Gregory the Theologian, *Orations* 45. 8, PG 36, 633AB, trans. Browne and Swallow (NPNF, vol. 7), Peabody, 2004, p. 425. See P. Nellas, "God allows death to exist but turns it against corruption and its cause, sin, and sets a boundary both to corruption and to sin. ... His original plan for man's eternal and blessed life in Him remains intact." *Deification in Christ*, p. 65.

[19] St. Cyril of Alexandria, *On the Incarnation of the Lord*, trans. S. Rose, in *Orthodox Dogmatic Theology*, Platina, 1984, pp. 158-159. "God permitted death in order that man should not remain forever in a living death." Metro. Hierotheos, *Life After Death*, p. 46.

"By allowing man to dress himself in biological life ..." writes Nellas, "[God] redirected death, and thus by death is put to death not man, but the corruption which clothes him. Death destroys this prison of life-in-corruption, and man ... is liberated through death."[20]

God provides us with opportunities to freely repent from sin and strive for true life in Christ, for which we are intended: "So here we see God's love for mankind. He expels man from Paradise so that he will not remain mortal forever, but may repent and at the suitable time, through the Incarnation, may ... overcome death ... So then, man's expulsion from Paradise was not a punishment by God, but an act of His love and philanthropy."[21]

Christ liberates human nature from the bonds of sin and death through His death and Resurrection. Furthermore, Christ empowers us, as living members of His Resurrected Body, with the means to defeat the forces of spiritual death, here and now. theosis

Through our personal participation in the ascetic, sacramental and liturgical life of Christ's Holy Church, we are led to spiritual therapy. Here, our spiritual illnesses are properly treated and healed. Death is a transient phenomenon. It is a momentary interim. When looking at death through the lens of Christ's Resurrection, we see it in an entirely different perspective.

---

[20] P. Nellas, *Deification in Christ*, p. 64.
[21] Metro. Hierotheos, *The Twelve Feasts of the Lord*, trans. Williams, Levadia, 2000, p. 371.

Resurrection

Belief in the resurrection of the human body is fundamental to the Orthodox Faith. It is a matter of faith alone. For many outside the Church, belief in the Resurrection appears irrational. So is our belief that God actually became man, or that bread and wine become the Body and Blood of Christ.

Our Church teaches that every human being who ever lived will be resurrected on the Last Day.[22] Each one of us, whether a believer in the Resurrection or not, will be resurrected to his own body. And we will be judged in our body, for how we lived and for what we did in these bodies while here on earth.[23]

The Apostle Paul teaches Christ, "will transform our lowly body that it may be conformed to His glorious body."[24] Our resurrected body will be our same body, but it will be glorified. It will be a spiritual body.[25]

---

[22] See John 5. 28-29.

[23] See St. Maximos the Confessor, "Our Lord and God Jesus Christ, showing His love for us, suffered for the whole of mankind and gave to all men an equal hope of resurrection, although each man determines his own fitness for glory or punishments." *Texts on Love* 1. 71, PG 90, 976C, trans. *The Philokalia* 2, London, 1981, p. 60.

[24] Phil. 3. 21.

[25] See 1 Cor. 15. 35, 42-44.

St. John Chrysostom writes, "It is the same, and not the same; the same, because the substance [οὐσία] is the same; but not the same, because this is more excellent, the substance [οὐσία] remaining the same but its beauty becoming greater, and the same body rising up new."[26]

St. Gregory Palamas elaborates, "When those who have lived here in a godly manner are separated from their bodies, they are not separated from God, and in the resurrection they will take their bodies with them to God, and in their bodies they will enter with inexpressible joy there where Jesus has preceded us, and in their bodies they will enjoy the glory that will be revealed in Christ."[27] He continues, "But this does not apply to those who live this present life in an unregenerate manner and who at death have no communion with God. For though all will be resurrected, yet the resurrection of each individual will be in accordance with his own inner state."[28]

Non-believers will also be resurrected, but their bodies will not be glorified. The bodies of the faithful, will be glorified, however, according to the condition of their souls.[29]

---

[26] St. John Chrysostom, *Homilies on First Corinthians* 41. 3, PG 61, 356-357, trans. T. Chambers (NPNF, vol. 12), Peabody, 2004, p. 250. See St. Isaac the Syrian, "That grace whereby we are resurrected after we have sinned is greater than the grace which brought us into being when we were not." *Ascetic Homilies* 51, trans. Holy Transfiguration Monastery, Brookline, 2011, p. 388.

[27] St. Gregory Palamas, *To the Nun Xeni* 15, PG 1052AB, trans. *The Philokalia* 4, p. 298.

[28] Ibid.

[29] See 1 Cor. 15. 41.

The deep reverence and respect the Orthodox Church has for the human body is based ultimately on the Incarnation of Christ. Not only are we uniquely created in the image of God,[30] but the Son of God has now assumed our human nature, with a real human body. He did not assume the nature of an angel, nor of any other created being. God became human.

And not only is the fullness of our nature—including our body—assumed by the Son of God, but it was also resurrected by Him after His voluntary death on the Holy Cross. Furthermore, forty days after His Resurrection, at His glorious Ascension,[31] Christ took His body with Him, so that His complete human nature—including His human body—now sits "at the right hand of the Father."[32] Christ will never cease being human.[33]

This is the same Body that the faithful are engrafted into through Holy Baptism: "For we are members of His body, of His flesh and His bones."[34]

---

[30] Gen. 1. 26.

[31] See Acts 1. 9-11 and Luke 24. 50, 51.

[32] The Nicene-Constantinopolitan Creed. See Mark 16. 19.

[33] See St. Gregory Palamas, "He ascended in glory ... and sat down on the right hand of the heavenly majesty, making our human substance share His own throne and divinity." *Homilies* 21. 12, ibid., p. 174.

[34] Eph. 5. 30. "Do you not know that your bodies are members of Christ?" 1 Cor. 6. 15. "Now you are the body of Christ, and members individually." 1 Cor. 12. 27.

This is the same Body believers partake in when receiving Holy Communion: "The bread which we break, is it not the communion of the body of Christ?"[35] ✓

We become the Body of Christ—not because we lose our own bodies—but because we conform to the likeness of Christ.[36] Our bodies are intended to become holy.[37] Together as one, our body and soul are saved and sanctified. Together as one, our body and soul will be resurrected into eternal life.

The Inherent Unity of Our Body and Soul

Man has a unique position in God's creation. Of all God's creatures, only man is both spiritual and physical. Man is spiritual by nature of his soul, as well as physical by nature of his body. Like the holy angels, there is an obvious spiritual aspect to human existence. And like other creatures of the material world, we too have a physical body. Man alone, within the entire universe, was created with both a spiritual soul and a material body.

---

[35] 1 Cor. 10. 16. "This is My body which is given for you; do this in remembrance of Me." Luke 22. 19.
[36] See St. Maximos the Confessor, "We are said to be the body of Christ. We do not become this body through the loss of our own bodies; nor again because Christ's body ... is divided into members; but rather because we conform to the likeness of the Lord's flesh by shaking off the corruption of sin." *Two Hundred Texts on Theology* 2. 84, PG 90, 1164C, trans. ibid., p. 158.
[37] See Rom. 12. 1 and 1 Cor. 6. 19.

An organic inter-connection exists between our soul and body. The afflictions of our soul affect our body.[38] Likewise, bodily afflictions affect our soul. They can break our spirit if we let them, leading to despondency, depression and despair. On the other hand, bodily afflictions can provide opportunities for spiritual growth and the purification of our soul.

The condition of our body affects the condition of our soul, and *vice versa*: "Some passions enter the body by way of the soul, and some work in the opposite way,"[39] states St. John Climacus.

A healthy soul also affects one's body in a positive way. St. Paisios speaks from his personal experience, "It is possible for one to always have the flame of divine love in his heart. I constantly had that heavenly sweetness. My whole body was burning and my bones were like flaming candles."[40]

---

[38] "With stress, pressure, distress, anxiety, an ulcer or cancer comes about. When there are confusions in our soul, these have influence on our body and our health suffers." St. Porphyrios, *Wounded by Love*, trans. J. Raffan, Limni, 2005, p. 229.

[39] St. John Climacus, *The Ladder of Divine Ascent* 15, trans. Luibheid and Russell, New York, 1982, p. 183. "Pride in a person can be seen in the clothes he wears, the way he walks and the way he talks." St. Paisios of Mount Athos, *Passions and Virtues*, trans. P. Chamberas, Thessalonica, 2016, p. 67.

[40] St. Paisios of Mount Athos, *Passions and Virtues*, p. 219. See ibid., p. 204. See also St. Gregory Palamas, "According to the measure of its own progress [the soul] communicates its joy to the body too ..." *The Declaration of the Holy Mountain* 6, PG 150, 1233B, trans. *The Philokalia* 4, pp. 423-424.

Participation in God's grace is not limited to one's heart and soul. Divine grace affects the *entire* man, including the physical body: "The heart directs and governs all the other organs of the body. And when grace pastures the heart, it rules over all the members ... This is how grace penetrates throughout all parts of the body."[41]

Our Body Participates in Prayer

The whole man, body and soul, is created for holiness. Our entire person—body and soul—participates in prayer.

Our body is created for prayer. We pray bowing our heads and bending our knees; by prostrating and crossing ourselves. We pray kneeling and standing; by kissing icons and lighting candles. We read and chant our prayers.

Prostrations are an excellent illustration of how the body participates in prayer. St. Porphyrios explains the vital role of prostrations: "When prostrations are made for Christ, grace works directly on the soul ... We acknowledge our lowliness and display our respect in a tangible way. With prostrations the Christian is humbled, and this helps for the grace of God to come upon him. ..."

---

[41] St. Macarios of Egypt, *The Fifty Spiritual Homilies* 15. 20, PG 34, 589AB, trans. G. Maloney, New York, 1992, p. 116. See St. Paisios, "The detoxification from the passions and the purification of the soul are discernible even in the flesh, which is also purified because the purification begins with the heart. Through the circulation of the blood, the heart transmits its spirituality to the flesh, sanctifying the whole person." *Passions and Virtues*, p. 166.

Prostrations are a sacrifice and offering—an offering of love and worship. And the whole person participates in this worship, both body and soul."[42]

Regarding the practice of kneeling, St. Isaac the Syrian writes, "Whenever you find it delightful to kneel in prayer, do not be carried off by the thought to put an end to it. Would that this were never cut short for as long as you are in this life!"[43]

Our body not only participates in prayer—it enriches our prayers. Our prayers are more effective when accompanied with ascetic self-denial and sacrifice: "One should not seek his own ease, his convenience. Self-denial is needed first ... for when self-renunciation exists, then God gives one His Grace. ... The help one receives from God is analogous to the sacrifice and prayer he does for his fellow human beings."[44]

---

[42] St. Porphyrios, *Wounded by Love*, p. 169.
[43] St. Isaac the Syrian, *Ascetical Homilies* 64, trans. HTM, 2011, p. 449. "Who is the man who knows that delightful bending of the knees, when ... the body is still, resting upon the knees? Blessed is he who partakes of these things continually!" *Ascetical Homilies* 22, ibid., p. 237.
[44] St. Paisios, *Passions and Virtues*, p. 57.

Our body plays a fundamental role within our spiritual lives. What we do *to* our body and what we do *with* our body—what we put on it and in it—directly affects our spiritual health. This pertains not only to positive practices such as fasting, prostrations and the purification of our passions, but also in a negative way, our participation in the passions of gluttony, drunkenness and sexual promiscuity, to whatever degree, adversely affect our spiritual lives. They repel divine grace and impede our pursuit of prayer.

The Sanctification of the Human Body

The sanctification of the human body results from the sanctification of our soul.[45] When our soul is sanctified, it directly affects our body: "In the spiritual man, the grace of the Spirit, *transmitted to the body* through the soul, *grants to the body* also the experience of things divine, and allows it the same blessed experiences as the soul undergoes."[46]

---

[45] See St. Maximos, "The body is deified along with the soul through its own corresponding participation in the process of deification." *Two Hundred Texts on Theology* 2. 88, PG 90, 1168A, trans. *The Philokalia* 2, p. 160.

[46] St. Gregory Palamas, *Defense of the Hesychasts*, 2. 2. 12, trans. N. Gendle (under the title *The Triads*), New York, 1983, p. 51 [italics mine]. He adds, "Spiritual dispositions are stamped upon the body as a consequence of the gifts of the Spirit that exist in the soul of those advancing on the spiritual path ... through [the soul] the dispositions and activities of the body are also sanctified, since body and soul share a conjoint existence." *The Declaration of the Holy Mountain* 6, PG 150, 1233D, trans. *The Philokalia* 4, pp. 423-424.

The word 'to sanctify' (ἀγιάζω) is referred to throughout the liturgical life of the Orthodox Church. The term may appear on its own or with specific reference to either the soul or body. At other times, it refers directly to both soul and body. Its use is so wide-spread, only a few examples are cited here.

To begin with, the Apostle Paul writes to the Thessalonians, "Now may the God of peace Himself sanctify (ἀγιάσαι) you completely."[47] And also to the Corinthians, "But you were washed, but you were sanctified (ἡγιάσθητε), but you were justified in the name of the Lord Jesus ..."[48] This same phrase is referred to in the Mystery of Holy Chrismation, "Thou art justified. Thou art illumined. Thou art sanctified."[49]

In the Divine Liturgy, 'sanctify' (ἀγιάζω) or 'sanctification' (ἀγιασμός) is referred to from beginning to end. During the Service of Preparation or *Proskomide*, after the priest has veiled and censed the Gifts, he prays that Christ, "... be our Savior and Redeemer ... blessing and sanctifying (ἀγιάζοντα) us."[50] And at the Prayer of Thanksgiving, "For Thou art our sanctification (ἀγιασμός) ..."[51]

---

[47] 1 Thess. 5. 23.
[48] 1 Cor. 6. 11.
[49] The Mystery of Holy Chrismation, Prayer Before the Tonsure, *Service Book*, trans. I. Hapgood, Englewood, 1975, p. 284.
[50] The Service of Preparation (Proskomide), Priestly Prayer at the Censing of the Gifts, *Service Book*, ibid., p. 75.
[51] The Liturgy of St. John Chrysostom, Priestly Prayer at the Litany of Thanksgiving, *A Prayer Book for Orthodox Christians*, trans. Holy Transfiguration Monastery, Brookline, 2014, p. 132.

Also at the conclusion of the Liturgy, the priest prays, "O Lord, Who blesses them that bless Thee, and sanctifies (ἀγιάζων) them that put their trust in Thee ... sanctify (ἀγίασον) them that love the beauty of Thy house."[52]

Elsewhere in our liturgical life, the term 'sanctify' refers directly to both soul and body. During the Mystery of Holy Unction, we chant, "O Christ Who ... hast sanctified (ἀγιάσας) both our souls and bodies from on high ..."[53]

In the Liturgy of the Presanctified Gifts, at the Litany Before the Lord's Prayer, the priest prays quietly, "Sanctify (ἀγίασον) all our souls and bodies with the sanctification (ἀγιασμῷ) which cannot be taken away ..."[54]

In the Prayers Before Holy Communion, at the Second Prayer, we pray, "Let these holy Gifts be unto my healing, and purification ... and sanctification (ἀγιασμόν) of both soul and body ..."[55]

---

[52] The Liturgy of St. John Chrysostom, *A Prayer Book for Orthodox Christians*, trans. HTM, p. 133.
[53] The Mystery of Holy Unction, *Service Book*, Canticle 5, trans. Hapgood, p. 336.
[54] The Liturgy of the Presanctified Gifts, Litany Before the Lord's Prayer, trans. St. Tikhon's Monastery Press, *Service Books of the Orthodox Church* vol. 2, 1984, p. 148.
[55] Prayers Before Holy Communion, Second Prayer (St. Basil), *A Prayer Book for Orthodox Christians*, trans. HTM, p. 358. The numbering of Pre-Communion Prayers differs slightly in some manuals.

At the Third Prayer, "Let the live coal of Thine all-holy Body and Thy precious Blood be unto sanctification (ἁγιασμόν) and enlightenment and strengthening of my humble soul and body ... O Master, sanctify (ἁγίασον) my soul and body, my mind and heart ..."[56]

At the Fifth Prayer, we pray that our participation in Holy Communion be unto our "... sanctification (ἁγιασμόν) and enlightenment ... and health of both soul and body ..."[57]

Not only before Holy Communion, but also afterwards, at the Prayers of Thanksgiving, we pray that "... these Thy dread and life-creating Mysteries [be] for the benefit and sanctification of our souls and bodies ..."[58]

From these few liturgical texts, we see our body's potential for sanctification in Christ. And holy relics are the clearest manifestation of how the human body can be sanctified through divine grace.

---

[56] Prayers Before Holy Communion, Third Prayer (St. John Chrysostom), *A Prayer Book for Orthodox Christians*, pp. 359-360.
[57] Prayers Before Holy Communion, Fifth Prayer (St. John Chrysostom), ibid., pp. 361-362.
[58] Thanksgiving Prayers After Holy Communion, First Prayer, ibid., p. 374.

Holy Relics

Since the time of the first persecutions, Christians honored relics of holy martyrs. For this reason, pagan persecutors often disposed the bodies of martyrs by throwing them into the sea, so their relics would not fall into the hands of Christians who would honor and venerate them.[59] In many cases relics became, by God's grace, sources of countless miracles and healings.

Once the early persecutions ended, Christians continued gathering and preserving the relics of their saints. This gave rise to the practice of exhumation, or reverent removal of relics from graves. These relics were then solemnly placed within altars of local churches, often built in their honor.

As early as the fourth century, at the consecration of a church, the practice of placing relics within the holy altar became widespread. It was formally approved and mandated in 787 by the seventh canon of the Seventh Ecumenical Council.[60] This practice was based on the ancient Christian custom of celebrating the Holy Eucharist directly over tombs of the martyrs, stemming from the first centuries of the Church.[61]

---

[59] See *Θρησκευτικὴ καὶ Ἠθικὴ Ἐγκυκλοπαιδεία,* vol. 8, Athens, 1966, p. 212.

[60] "And if any bishop from this time forward is found consecrating a temple without holy relics, he shall be deposed, as a transgressor of the ecclesiastical traditions." *The Seven Ecumenical Councils,* The Seventh Ecumenical Council, *Canon* 7, trans. Percival (NPNF, vol. 14), p. 560.

[61] See *Θρησκευτικὴ καὶ Ἠθικὴ Ἐγκυκλοπαιδεία,* vol. 8, p. 214.

This practice is continued today. At the Service for the Consecration of an Orthodox Church, the local bishop seals relics within the holy altar, so that the Holy Eucharist is still celebrated over the relics of martyrs and saints, even today.[62]

Holy relics play a fundamental role within the life of the Orthodox Church. Interestingly, several early heretical groups disapproved of their veneration,[63] as do the majority of contemporary Protestant confessions.

Today, throughout the Orthodox world, many holy relics are known as sources for healing, exorcisms, and other miracles: "The presence of the grace of God in the holy relics is shown in a variety of ways. Sometimes it is by their incorruption, sometimes by their fragrance, sometimes by miracles, and so forth, and it is perceived by those who have faith and pure spiritual senses."[64]

Countless instances are found throughout the Lives of Saints. St. Haralambos († *circa* 194-211) is one example: "The skull of St. Haralambos is kept at the Monastery of St. Stephen at Meteroa. The fragments of his holy relics, which are to be found in many places in Greece and elsewhere, accomplish frequent miracles and have made St. Haralambos ... especially dear to the people of Greece."[65]

---

[62] In particular instances, there may be certain exceptions.
[63] See Θρησκευτικὴ καὶ Ἠθικὴ Ἐγκυκλοπαιδεία, vol. 8, p. 212.
[64] Metro. Hierotheos, *The Person in the Orthodox Tradition*, trans. E. Williams, Levadia, 1988, p. 247.
[65] *The Synaxarion* vol. 3, February 10, Ormylia, 2001, p. 466.

Relics are often known to emit fragrant myrrh. A notable example is St. Demetrius the Myrrh-gusher (†306) the patron Saint of Thessalonica. His holy relics still emit fragrant myrrh today: "It was God's will that the grace with which He filled Saint Demetrius should remain active even after his death. This is why He caused to flow from his body a *myron* [fragrant myrrh] with a delightful scent, which had the property of healing all who took it as an unction, with faith in the intercession of the Saint."[66]

Other saints are known for emitting myrrh at the moment of their death. Examples include St. Theodora of Thessalonica (†892): "When she fell asleep in peace in 892, in the presence of the whole community [of nuns] her aged and wrinkled face was suddenly irradiated with the bloom of youth, filling the room with heavenly fragrance."[67]

Also St. Luke the New Martyr (†1802): For three days as his body hung from the gallows, "no insects dared to approach him and, moreover, a lovely fragrance was released around him, witnessing to the favor that he had found with God."[68]

In many instances, bodies of saints remain entirely incorrupt. In other words, their bodies have not decomposed. Their skin still remains even hundreds of years after their deaths. A few examples include Sts. Spyridon, Gerasimos and Dionysios.

---

[66] *The Synaxarion* vol. 1, October 26, Ormylia, 1998, p. 483.
[67] *The Synaxarion* vol. 4, April 5, Ormylia, 2003, p. 340.
[68] *The Synaxarion* vol. 4, March 23, ibid., p. 218.

St. Spyridon of Corfu (†348): "His body became an inex-
haustible source of miracles and healings for the faithful
... [It] was taken secretly to Corfu (1456) where it has
been kept ever since, miraculously incorrupt. So many
miracles have been wrought through it for particular persons as well as for the population as a whole—deliver-
ances from epidemics and foreign invasion—that St. Spyridon is venerated as the principle protector of Corfu."[69]

St. Gerasimos of Kephalonia (†1579): "Until the present
day, the body of St. Gerasimos remains complete and incorrupt, as if he were asleep. It distills a heavenly fragrance and works many miracles. The Saint has become
the patron of the island of Kephalonia, the protector of all
the inhabitants ... Particularly notable is his power to de-
liver the possessed, who are brought from all quarters into
the presence of his relics."[70]

St. Dionysios of Zakynthos (†1622): At the exhumation of
his relics, the Abbot and brethren of the monastery "were
surprised to find his whole body miraculously incorrupt
and exhaling a fragrant perfume ... In 1717, his precious
relic was translated to the cathedral of Zakynthos where it
is venerated with devotion by all the inhabitants of the island. St. Dionysios has shown to this day that he is well
and truly alive by a multitude of signs, miracles and appa-
ritions, so that he is regarded as the principal protector
and patron of Zakynthos."[71]

---

[69] *The Synaxarion* vol. 2, December 12, Ormylia, 2001, p. 396.
[70] *The Synaxarion* vol. 1, October 20, ibid., p. 437.
[71] *The Synaxarion* vol. 2, December 17, ibid., p. 454.

On Mount Athos, at Vatopedi, St. John Chrysostom's skull still retains not only skin, but also his entire left ear. His incorrupt right hand is at Philotheou. The incorrupt left hand of St. Mary Magdalene is found at Simonos Petras. The incorrupt leg of St. Fotini the Samaritan woman is at Iveron.

Holy relics authenticate the truth of our Church's teaching on the deification of human nature.[72]

Conclusion

The Orthodox Church upholds the human body in the highest regard. No world religion, nor Christian confession, honors the human body with such veneration as the Orthodox Church.

This great reverence for the human body informs many Orthodox teachings relating to contemporary ethical issues such as abortion, cremation and sexuality.

This deep respect for the human body extends to all of God's material creation. We are created, and we are called, to live as a high priest, offering creation back to our Creator in gratitude—beginning with our own bodies.

Our body is an integral part of our spiritual lives. As human beings, how we view and what we do to our body can lead to either salvation or separation from God; to sanctification or damnation; genuine spiritual *life*, or eternal spiritual death.

---

[72] See Met. Hierotheos, *The Person in the Orthodox Tradition*, p. 247.

As Orthodox Christians, we look beyond the temporary tragedy of bodily death, anticipating our resurrection in Christ, where our body is destined to participate in His divine grace and glory.

We must not constrict our body to this earthly existence, to this worldly sphere, where it remains separated and estranged from God. The human body must be seen in light of our ultimate purpose and true spiritual potential.

Outside the light of the Resurrection of Christ, human existence has no true meaning—life has no lasting value.

In the words of Elder Vasileios of Mount Athos: "It is the end, the conclusion, the Resurrection that throws light on everything. Without the Resurrection, everything is obscure and meaningless ... Without the Resurrection and freedom from death, man is a defective creature. He does not live, he vegetates. He withers and is obliterated within time."[73]

---

[73] Archim. Vasilieos, *The Divine Liturgy as a Theophany of the Holy Trinity*, trans. E. Theokritoff, Montreal, 2015, p. 15.

Chapter Two: Human Freedom

"Freedom ... is both dangerous and salvific."

Elder Vasileios of Mount Athos

Preliminary Points

For many people, freedom appears antithetical to Orthodox spiritual life. For example, the Orthodox Church prescribes fasting, abstinence, long liturgical services, the keeping of the commandments and obedience. Taken out of context, one might have the impression that personal freedom has little or no role within one's life in the Orthodox Church. As we will see, such a view is misinformed.

Why is freedom so important to our lives? Why are we willing to fight and die for freedom? What *is* freedom?

The Oxford English Dictionary defines freedom as, "Exemption or release from slavery or imprisonment, liberation from bondage, independence, liberty of action, or the power of self-determination."[1] In this sense, freedom is the ability to direct our actions and make voluntary choices without constraint.

---

[1] *The Oxford English Dictionary* vol. 6, Oxford, 1989, p. 164.

Another question: Why are only human beings free? Why do no other creatures on earth have this same gift as we do? Of course, animals in the wild are born with a certain sense of freedom. But their behavior is more or less constrained to instinct. This is not the same as our power of self-determination and the ability to freely make moral decisions. Only human beings are born with free choice and the ability to freely direct our own lives.

A further question: Just what are we really free for anyway—freedom for what? Is it freedom to do whatever we want, or to buy or try whatever we want? In contemporary western society, freedom and sin are often interwoven. From the secular world-view, freedom involves free choice to pursue any pleasure we wish.

Spiritual Freedom

In the Orthodox Church, however, true freedom is freedom from bondage to unhealthy habits and worldly attachments. Freedom liberates us from those pleasures and passions that often enslave us. In *The Philokalia*, we read, "A man is free if he is not a slave to sensual pleasure. ... If you wish, you are a slave of the passions, and if you so wish, you are free to not yield to the passions. For God created you with free-will."[2]

---

[2] St. Anthony the Great, *On the Character of Men* 56 and 67, trans. *The Philokalia* 1, pp. 337 and 339.

In a spiritual sense, we are truly free only when liberated from sinful passions separating us from God's grace. Only then are we truly free to become the person we are created to be. This spiritual freedom is summed up by the Apostle Paul, "Stand fast therefore in the liberty by which Christ has made us free, and do not be entangled again with a yoke of bondage."[3] Referring to this 'yoke of bondage', St. Paul lists various 'works of the flesh', such as adultery, fornication, hatred, jealousy, envy and drunkenness.[4] These are derived ultimately from our fallen passions.

Passions and Virtues

St. Maximos the Confessor defines passion as an impulse of the soul that goes against, or is contrary to, our true nature.[5] A passion is a chronic or habitual misuse of human nature, such as pride and self-love.[6] Self-love is obsession with one's 'self'. Closely related to self-love is the passion of pride—excessive preoccupation with ourselves and our accomplishments.

---

[3] Gal. 5. 1. "All things are lawful for me, but all things are not helpful. All things are lawful for me, but I will not be brought under the power of any." 1 Cor. 6. 12.

[4] See Gal. 5. 19-21.

[5] "Passion is an impulse of the soul contrary to nature." St Maximos the Confessor, *Texts on Love* 2. 16, PG 90, 988D, trans. ibid., p. 67.

[6] The original Greek word for self-love is φιλαυτία (philautia).

Other major passions include greed, gluttony, anger and lust.[7] There is also the passion of despair, the most fatal of all, since it is a loss of all faith and hope in God.[8] These are some of the main passions that separate us from God and from each other.

Every passion has a corresponding virtue opposing and oppressing it. Virtue is "the conscious union of human weakness with divine strength."[9] Man approaches God and draws closer to Him through the pursuit and acquisition of spiritual virtues.[10] The primary virtue is self-less love, which entails love for God and love for neighbor.[11] Other major virtues include faith, hope, humility, gratitude, gentleness and chastity.

Virtues are antidotes for passions. The antidote for self-love is love for God and others. The antidote for pride is humility. Greed is off-set by gratitude for what we have, gluttony by self-control (such as fasting), and the passion of lust by the practice of chastity. Anger is defeated by gentleness; despair through the virtue of hope.

---

[7] For similar classifications of the major passions see Evagrius, *Practicus* 6 and St. John Cassian, *On the Eight Vices*. For a discussion on the list of passions in St. John Climacus, see the introduction by K. Ware in *The Ladder of Divine Ascent*, ibid., pp. 62-66.

[8] "To despair is to inflict death on oneself." St. John Climacus, *The Ladder of Divine Ascent* 5, PG 88, 780B, trans. ibid., p. 130.

[9] St. Maximos the Confessor, *Various Texts on Theology* 3. 79, PG 90, 1293D, trans. *The Philokalia* 2, p. 230.

[10] See St. John Damascene, *On the Virtues and Vices*, trans. *The Philokalia* 2, p. 341.

[11] See Matt. 22. 37-40 and 1 Cor. 13. 13.

Virtues, however, are more than antidotes for passions. Virtues manifest our true human nature. They truly set us free. Virtues are in fact natural to us, while passions are unnatural: "It is not food that is evil but gluttony, not the begetting of children but unchastity, not material things but avarice ... This being so, it is only the misuse of things that is evil ..."[12]

It is not simply healing from our passions that make us Christ-like. Rather, it is acquiring spiritual virtues.

Christ—The God-Man

We have an exalted place in God's creation. Man alone is uniquely created in the image and likeness of God.[13] Man is in fact God's masterpiece. God created the entire universe for us: "For man's sake God has created everything; earth and heaven and the beauty of the stars."[14]

The differences between our Church's view of man and that of contemporary culture are astounding: "So great was the honor and providential care which God bestowed upon man that He brought the entire sensible world into being before him and for his sake."[15]

---

[12] St. Maximos, *Texts on Love* 3. 4, PG 90, 1017CD, ibid., p. 83.
[13] See Gen. 1. 26.
[14] St. Anthony the Great, *On the Character of Men* 133, ibid., p. 349.
[15] St. Gregory Palamas, *Natural Chapters* 24, PG 150, 1136D, trans. *The Philokalia* 4, p. 356. See St. Nicholas Cabasilas, *Homily on the Annunciation* 6.

Not only is this material world created for man, but even the Kingdom of Heaven is also prepared for us: "Come, you blessed of My Father, inherit the kingdom prepared for you from the foundation of the world."[16]

In *The Philokalia* we read, "Only to man does God listen. Only to man does God manifest Himself. God loves man and, wherever man may be, God too is there. Man alone is counted worthy to worship God. ... For man's sake God transforms [μεταμορφοῦται] Himself."[17]

This 'transformation' is the Incarnation of Christ.

We comprehend the ultimate purpose of our lives only in the person of Christ, the God who became man. Only in Christ do we find our true identity as human beings. In the person of Christ, God not only became man, but man is called to participate in divine life. Christ is the key unlocking the mystery of the human person.[18]

Our short lifespan is a unique opportunity, an opportunity to attain to the life and likeness of Christ. Life is not about 'me'.[19] Life is about Christ.

---

[16] Matt. 25. 34.

[17] St. Anthony the Great, *On the Character of Men* 132, trans. *The Philokalia* 1, p. 349.

[18] "No one could ever know God, or man, fully, as it is given us to know through Christ. He made manifest to us both the Heavenly Father and man as he was intended before the creation of the world. The Lord Jesus Christ is absolute ontological Truth." Archim. Sophrony, *On Prayer,* trans. R. Edmonds, Essex, 1996, p. 84.

[19] Baby Boomers are often referred to as the 'Me Generation'. See T. Wolfe, "The 'Me' Decade", *New York Magazine*, August 23, 1976.

Christ created each of us, everyone who ever lived. And Christ calls each of us, to become like Him, in a unique and personal way.

This differs from the values promoted in contemporary society, where the focus is typically centered on one's 'self'. We are programmed to obsess on our individual self, at the expense of our relationship with God and others. When we focus on our *self*, we can become, over time, slaves of our own selves—slaves of self-love. We then actually lose our gift of freedom. We also lose our true identity as human beings.

Man is Created for Spiritual Growth

Man was not originally created in a condition of complete spiritual perfection. Adam and Eve were created as spiritual infants. They were created for spiritual growth. St. Irenaeus teaches while all the animals were fully developed from the moment of their creation—man alone was created a spiritual infant, "and it was necessary for him to reach full development by growing in this way."[20] Not only Adam and Eve, but all of us are created to grow spiritually, using our God-given freedom.

---

[20] St. Irenaeus, *On the Apostolic Preaching* 12, trans. J. Behr, Crestwood, 1997, p. 47. "Adam was created in a state of childlike simplicity and innocence; an infant spiritually and morally, and incapable of clearly discerning good from evil." Ibid. See Theophilus, *To Autolycus* 2. 25.

Whatever spiritual progress we attain, whatever Christ-like virtues we acquire, it always depends directly on our free will, just as much as it depends on God: "This being was placed in paradise ... [and] honored with self-determination so that the good would belong to the one who chose it no less than to the one who provided its seeds."[21]

God respects human freedom so much that He permits the outcomes of our free choices, good and bad. Unfortunately, rather than choosing to actualize our spiritual potential, too often we activate our self-centered pride. The purpose of our life and our primary focus are now tragically centered on our *self*.

In this fallen state, our tendency is to cultivate un-natural attachment to material possessions and bodily passions: "The bodily passions ... feed the pride in the human person that satisfies them. His exclusively material needs and passions will be a source of pride justified by his proud claim to be autonomous."[22]

We take great pride in our lusts and carnal passions. We become so proud of our passions that we even idolize and identify with them.

---

[21] St. Gregory the Theologian, *Orations* 45. 8, PG 36, 632CD, trans. N. Harrison, p. 167. "For that which is done by force is not an act of virtue." St. John Damascene, *Exact Exposition* 2.12, PG 94, 924B, trans. F. Chase, Washington DC, 1958, p. 236.
[22] D. Staniloae, *The Experience of God*, vol. 2, trans. Ionita and Barringer, Brookline, 2000, p. 171.

According to Elder Sophrony, "The man who is not suffi-
ciently attentive within himself falls under the influence
of an intrusive thought and becomes enslaved. By heeding
the intrusive idea man comes to resemble—even identifies with—the spirit of the intrusive thought, and the energy contained in it."[23] This in turn leads to further aliena-
tion from God, our neighbors and ourselves.

Three Conditions of Human Nature

The Church Fathers distinguish three different states or
conditions of human nature. Human life can be lived *according* to nature (κατὰ φύσιν), *contrary* to nature (παρὰ
φύσιν), or *above* nature (ὑπὲρ φύσιν).[24]

Human life lived *according* to nature is the original condition of Adam and Eve as they lived before the Fall. This
is how God first intended mankind to live. This is referred
to as man's *pre-fallen* state.

The second condition is life lived *contrary* to nature. This
is our fallen nature, our present state. In our fallen condition, we live contrary to, or against, our nature as originally
intended by God.

---

[23] Archim. Sophrony, *St. Silouan the Athonite*, p. 136.
[24] E.g., St. John Damascene, *Exact Exposition* 2. 30, trans. F. Chase,
p. 264; St. Maximos the Confessor, *Various Texts on Theology* 1. 75
and 4. 20, trans. *The Philokalia* 2, pp. 181 and 240; St. Isaac the Syrian, *Ascetical Homilies* 3; St. Gregory of Sinai, *On Commandments
and Doctrines* 68-69, trans. *The Philokalia* 4, p. 224; St. Mark the Ascetic, *No Righteousness by Works* 90, trans. *The Philokalia* 1, p. 132.

And the third condition is human life lived *above* nature. This is the fullness of the life in Christ for which we are ultimately created. Human nature is now *deified* through union with the divine nature of the Incarnated Christ. This is what our saints attain to, by divine grace.

An excellent example of someone living contrary to nature but through repentance and purification reached life *above* nature, and became deified and holy, is St. Mary of Egypt.

From a very early age she gave herself over to passions of the flesh. For over seventeen years she lived a life of carnal lust and sexual pleasure, even refusing money from the men she went with. But later in life, by God's grace and her great repentance, she abandoned her life contrary to nature and attained to holiness. She went on to become a great saint of our Church.

In his letter to the Romans, the Apostle Paul describes the frustration of living in this fallen state: "I am carnal, sold under sin. For what I am doing, I do not understand. For what I will to do, that I do not practice; but what I hate, that I do. ... For the good that I will to do, I do not do; but the evil I will not to do, that is what I practice."[25]

St. Paul refers to the dysfunction of our fallen nature. The good things we intend to do, we don't do; and the very things we do not want to do, and are trying to avoid, this is exactly what we do!

---

[25] Romans 7. 14-15, 19.

St. Paul goes on to describe how Christ can empower our free-will to actually make the right and positive choices our hearts truly desire. Through the power of repentance, we can turn from the sins and passions of our fallen state and acquire the virtues of our natural condition.

"While we abide in the natural state, we abide in virtue," writes St. John Damascene, "but when we deviate from the natural state, that is from virtue, we come into an unnatural state and dwell in wickedness. Repentance is the returning from the unnatural to the natural state, from the devil to God, through discipline and effort."[26]

Human Life According to Nature

Life before the Fall was in accordance with our true nature as first created by God. Adam's only desire was for God: "There [in the Garden] he had the indwelling God as a dwelling place and wore Him as a glorious garment. He was wrapped about with His grace...he rejoiced in the enjoyment of that one most sweet fruit which is the contemplation of God, and by this he was nourished."[27]

---

[26] St. John Damascene, *Exact Exposition* 2. 30, PG 94, 976A, trans. S. Salmond (NPNF, vol. 9), Peabody, 2004, p. 43. "We have it in our power either to abide in virtue and follow God, Who calls us into ways of virtue, or to stray from paths of virtue, which is to dwell in wickedness, and to follow the devil who summons [us] but cannot compel us." Ibid.

[27] St. John Damascene, *Exact Exposition* 2. 11, PG 94, 916C, trans. F. Chase, p. 232.

St. Gregory of Nyssa writes, "He was naked of the covering of dead skins, and saw the face of God with easy fa-
miliarity. He ... only delighted in the Lord, and it was to
this end that he availed himself."[28]

St. Gregory Palamas refers to the pre-fallen state as one of
divine illumination: "Adam, before the Fall, also partici-
pated in this divine illumination and resplendence, and
because he was truly clothed in a garment of glory he was
not naked, nor was he unseemly by reason of his naked-
ness. He was far more richly adorned than those who now
deck themselves out with ... gold and brightly sparkling
jewels."[29]

Before the Fall, Adam and Eve lived in communion with
God, freely choosing to obey His will. They enjoyed the
presence of God. When they fell, they sought to hide from
God: "And they heard the sound of the Lord God walking
in the garden ... and Adam and his wife hid themselves
from the presence of the Lord God among the trees of the
garden. Then the Lord God called to Adam and said to
him, 'Where are you?' So [Adam] said, 'I heard Your voice
in the garden, and I was afraid because I was naked; and I
hid myself'."[30]

---

[28] St. Gregory of Nyssa, *On Virginity* 12, PG 46, 369-376C, trans. N.
Russell in *Deification in Christ*, p. 209.
[29] St. Gregory Palamas, *Natural Chapters* 67, PG 150, 1168D, trans.
The Philokalia 4, p. 377.
[30] Gen. 3. 8-10.

We are created to participate in divine life. In our fallen state, however, our goal is no longer focused on communion with God. When we sin, we likewise seek to hide from God, thinking we can separate ourselves from His presence.[31]

Human Life Contrary to Nature

We are created with an innate desire for God. When we convince ourselves that we have no need for God, we depersonalize ourselves. Our nature becomes dysfunctional. We desecrate the divine image in which we are created. We become inhumane, or even 'sub-human'.

Referring to the de-humanization of contemporary man, the beloved Serbian saint and theologian St. Justin (Popovich) shares these insightful words: "Without the God-man, man is in fact without a head ... Without the God-man, man does not exist; there is only less-than-man, half-man or no man at all. ... Without the God-man and independently of Him, man always risks the danger of becoming like the devil. ... Functioning independently of the God-man, man voluntarily reduces himself to a devil-like state of sin. ... We must not forget that the principal objective of the devil is to deprive man of his God-like potential ... to delete his divinity, and to thus transform [man] into a being similar to himself."[32]

---

[31] "One must be constantly aware of the presence of God. When one is aware of the presence of God ... it acts as a strong brake that keeps him from going astray." St. Paisios, *Passions and Virtues*, p. 287.

[32] St. Justin, *Orthodox Faith and Life in Christ*, trans. Gerostergios, Belmont, 1994, pp. 100-101.

The idea of man living apart from God, or having no need for God, is indeed a strange kind of fiction.[33] Modern man has made himself God—devolving himself into a monstrous caricature of God.

St. Justin also offers these thoughts: "In essence, man's fall consisted in the fact that man rebelled against the God-like characteristics of his being, he abandoned God ... and reduced himself to pure materiality, to pure man. With the first rebellion against God, man to a degree succeeded in driving God out of himself, out of his conscience, out of his will, and so is left with pure humanness, with pure ... humanism. Humanism is in fact the fundamental evil, the original evil of man. In the name of ... humanism, man has driven God out ... and is left entirely with himself and within himself."[34]

We tend to forget our fallen condition. Our fallen nature is governed by a dysfunctional will, filled with abnormal desires innately foreign to us, and leading us away from God. Apart from God, we lack authentic life. Apart from God, we strive to be human through our own endeavors and devices. This is the 'humanism' St. Justin refers to.

In our fallen state, there is often a tendency to look upon each other in terms of material gain or carnal pleasure. We are more inclined now to seek after worldly delights, rather than the divine life of God.

---

[33] See Yannaras, *The Freedom of Morality*, Crestwood, 1984, p. 30.
[34] St. Justin, *Man and the God-man*, Alhambra, 2009, p. 20.

"The fall," writes Dr. Elizabeth Theokritoff, "solidifies man in his animal nature. It makes him merely a top predator, a 'consumer'. The world around us is no longer a revelation ... but a resource to satisfy our appetite."[35]

Modern man is characterized more as a marketing or consumer statistic, and less than a unique and unrepeatable person created in the image and likeness of God.[36] We are de-personalizing ourselves, and our society, at an alarming rate. The dignity of the human person continues to diminish, with vast spiritual and social implications.

We have resigned ourselves to imitate the lowest spiritual ideals, with minimal moral expectations. The 'progressive' decay in the ethical values of each successive generation attests to these new standards. What was once socially unacceptable is now a new social norm.

Ongoing advancements in technology lead to further depersonalization. The explosion of the Internet and the advent of multiple forms of 'social' media contribute to the loss of genuine personal contact.

Many of us prefer texting instead of talking. We communicate more through virtual contact, in virtual reality, rather than through personal contact. In spite of all the continuing technological advancements, our daily lives are more complicated and oppressive than ever.

---

[35] E. Theokritoff, *Living in God's Creation*, Crestwood, 2009, p. 84.
[36] See Gen. 1. 26.

Stress, anxiety and depression lead to further despair and despondency. All these make us more vulnerable to self-destructive addictions.

Instead of living in communal love with one another, we now live as separate individuals in conflict and opposition. Human nature has become distorted and deformed. In our fallen state, our instinct now leads us to separate ourselves from each other. We divide and fragment our common nature.[37]

According to Vladimir Lossky, "A human person cannot realize the fullness to which he is called ... if he claims for himself a part of the nature, regarding it as his own particular good. ... He sets himself up as an individual, proprietor of his own nature, which he pits against the natures of others and regards as his 'me'."[38]

Fr. Dumitru Staniloae also writes: "Everyone has become spiritually impoverished ... Reduced in this way to his own self as the central reality ... the conscious creature could no longer understand even himself apart from his blind impulse toward biological satisfactions and carnal passions. Among humans, sin has introduced egoism, appetite for unessential things, spiritual weakness, spiritual death, followed by bodily death and everlasting death ...

---

[37] "Each person is isolated in his pride, whether physical or spiritual. From that position he fires off violent attacks, whether moral or material, against the soul and body of the other." Arch. Vasileios, *From the Old Adam to the New*, trans. E. Theokritoff, Montreal, 2008, p. 4.

[38] Lossky, *The Mystical Theology of the Eastern Church*, Crestwood, 1976, pp. 120-122. See Yannaras, *The Freedom of Morality*, p. 30.

"Once nature is degraded to being simply a means for satisfying bodily needs, it brings all kinds of difficulties."[39]

St. Paisios of Mount Athos offers this advice which is especially relevant for today: "People today have made their lives difficult, because they are not satisfied with a few things, but are constantly chasing after more and more material goods. But those who would like to live a genuine spiritual life must first of all be satisfied with a few things. When their life is simplified, without too many concerns ... not only will they be liberated from the worldly spirit, but they will also have plenty of time available for spiritual things. Otherwise, they will tire themselves out by trying to follow the fashion of the times; they will lose serenity and will only gain great anxiety."[40]

The Church Fathers compare fallen man with beasts and wild animals. St. Silouan writes: "How infirm is the soul! Without God's grace we are like cattle, but with grace great is man in the sight of God."[41] And St. Gregory of Sinai adds, "Through trespasses, we have become akin to beasts and have lost the natural blessings given us by God, becoming as beasts instead of reasoning beings, and animals instead of divine."[42]

---

[39] D. Staniloae, *The Experience of God* vol. 2, pp. 183-186.
[40] St. Paisios, *Family Life*, trans. P. Chamberas, ibid., p. 160.
[41] *Saint Silouan the Athonite*, p. 331.
[42] St. Gregory of Sinai, *Texts on Commandments and Dogmas* 9, *Writings from the Philokalia–Prayer of the Heart*, PG 150, 1241B, trans. Kadloubovsky and Palmer, London, 1992, p. 39.

St. John Chrysostom uses these powerful words, "When I see you robbing others, how am I to call you a human being and not a wolf? When I see you committing fornication, how am I to call you a human being and not a swine? When I see you with venom, how am I to call you a human being and not a snake? When I see you being a fool, how am I to call you a human being and not an ass?"[43]

When we don't seek Christ-like virtues, we become imprisoned by fallen passions. Slaves to the unnatural, we become less-than-human. It is from this unnatural condition that Christ saves us.

Human Life Above Nature: The Life in Christ

Christ saves us from life contrary to nature. Not only did He destroy death, He raises human nature to a higher condition. When the Son of God assumed our human nature, He imparted to it His divine and deifying grace: "The regeneration of human nature in Christ not only released it from the bonds of corruption and death, but raised it above its pre-fallen condition through deification."[44]

---

[43] St. John Chrysostom, *Homilies on the Psalms* 49. 16, trans. R. Hill, Brookline, 2003, p. 87.
[44] G. Mantzaridis, *The Deification of Man*, trans. L. Sherrard, Crestwood, 1984, p. 41.

In the person of Christ, human nature is deified, resurrected and ascended into the very life of the Holy Trinity. Human nature now 'sits at the right hand of the Father'.[45]

Through our union with Christ, we have the potential for deification, which is the highest state of human nature.[46]

The Church is the living extension of Christ's Body. His deified Body and Blood remain mystically present in His Holy Church. Through our personal participation in her ascetical, sacramental and liturgical life, we are engrafted into Christ: "It is fundamentally in the sacraments that we come into an ontological relationship with Christ Himself ... By becoming members of the Church through the sacraments, we are incorporated into Christ; through the sacraments, we become 'members of His body' and are made 'partakers of Christ', the Savior and deifier of our nature."[47]

---

[45] "Our human nature has become part of the mystery of the Holy Trinity, and that is a great gift which we do not even appreciate." Elder Thaddeus, *Our Thoughts Determine Our Lives*, trans. Smiljanic, Platina, 2010, p. 148.

[46] "The flesh of Christ, being the body of the Logos of God Incarnate, is the point of man's contact with God, and furnishes the way to the Kingdom of heaven ... Through the deification of Christ's human nature ... a 'new root' was created, capable of instilling life and incorruptibility into its shoots." Mantzaridis, *The Deification of Man*, p. 30. "Christ constitutes the real progenitor of a new humanity." Nellas, *Deification in Christ*, p. 112.

[47] J. Larchet, *Therapy of Spiritual Illness*, vol. 2, trans. Sprecher, Montreal, 2012, p. 27. "By baptism, chrismation, the divine eucharist and the rest of the spiritual life we are incorporated into Christ, we receive a ... Christocentric and Christ-like being." Nellas, *Deification in Christ*, p. 120.

Our participation in the Holy Eucharist is fundamental to our lives as Orthodox Christians. The Divine Eucharist is the means by which Christ's deified and deifying Blood is transfused into the believer's body.

St. Nicholas Cabasilas writes, "Christ infuses Himself into us and mingles Himself with us. He changes and transforms us into Himself, as a small drop of water is changed by being poured into an immense sea of ointment...we are mingled with Him in soul and united to Him in body and commingled in blood."[48]

While it is true we *receive* the Body of Christ within ourselves, it can also be said we are actually *being received* into Christ's deified Body: "While natural food is changed into him who feeds on it, and fish and bread and any other kind of food become human blood, here it is entirely opposite. The Bread of Life Himself changes him who feeds on Him and transforms and assimilates him into Himself."[49]

We are not merely saved from hell. We have the potential to be sanctified and made holy—to be deified by grace in Christ. We become living members of His deified and resurrected Body through our personal participation in the ascetic, sacramental and liturgical life of His Holy Church.

---

[48] St. Nicholas Cabasilas, *The Life in Christ* 4. 6 and 4. 10, PG 150, 593C and 601D, trans. C. Catanzaro, Crestwood, 1974, pp. 123 and 129. See *The Prayers of Thanksgiving After Holy Communion*, Prayer of St. Simeon Metaphrastes, "Consume me not, O My Creator, but instead enter into my members, my veins, my heart ..." St. Tikhon's Monastery Press, South Canaan, 1984, p. 187.
[49] St. Nicholas Cabasilas, *The Life in Christ* 4. 8, PG 150, 597B, p. 126.

Christ comes to live within His saints and holy people, who 'put on Christ'[50] and who truly live *in* Christ.[51]

We find such men and women who attained the life in Christ above nature within the lives of our Saints. The life of St. Seraphim of Sarov (†1833) is an excellent example. He was filled with such divine love and joy that every day was Pascha. He greeted all he met, regardless of the time of year, with a warm-hearted 'Christ is Risen, my joy!'

St. Paisios of Mount Athos (†1994), a contemporary saint attaining holiness in our own day, acquired the greatest spiritual gifts of prayer and healing. He was also beloved for his sharp wit and sense of humor, bringing heart-felt smiles to those seeking his guidance and advice.

Becoming Christ-like does not mean our saints shed their nature or discard their personalities. The opposite is true. To become holy is to become truly human. Holiness is found among our saints who have fulfilled their true personhood by putting on Christ—through the life in Christ— living within His Holy Church.

---

[50] See Gal. 3. 27.
[51] See Gal. 2. 20.

Conclusion: The Synergy of Grace and Freedom

Man strives toward participation in divine life as a co-worker with God. The proper theological term for this joint participation is synergy (συνέργεια), which means working with or working together.[52] As we strive to work out our salvation in Christ, there is a co-operation between human freedom and divine grace.

The thought that divine grace would somehow eliminate our effort is rejected by the Orthodox Church. For the Orthodox, there is no conflict between divine grace and human freedom. Our free will in working out our salvation is paramount. St. Mark the Ascetic summarizes the Orthodox view: "Grace has been given mystically to those who have been baptized into Christ; and it becomes active within them to the extent that they actively observe the commandments. Grace never ceases to help us secretly; but to do good—as far as lies in our power—depends on us."[53]

---

[52] See *A Patristic Greek Lexicon*, ed. Lampe, Oxford, 1961, p. 1323.

[53] St. Mark the Ascetic, *On Those Who Think That They are Made Righteous by Works* 61, PG 65, 937D, trans. *The Philokalia* 1, p. 130. See Elder Sophrony, "God constantly pursues man, and so soon as man manifests his own aspiration towards good and to putting good into actual practice, grace is already on the threshold. Yet the action or reaction of grace does not depend on man's will. Grace comes and goes according to the will of God Whose freedom is absolute and Who is subject to no compulsion." *St. Silouan the Athonite*, pp. 38-39.

It is important to point out another term the Church Fathers use when referring to our unique capacity to freely choose the life in Christ. This is *proairesis* (προαίρεσις), meaning "faculty of free choice", "deliberative choice" or "the ability to think things over and then to choose."[54]

St. Maximos uses *proairesis* in the context of choosing not to sin, "For just as Christ in His manhood was sinless by nature both in flesh and in soul, so we too who believe in Him, and have clothed ourselves in Him through the Spirit, can be without sin in Him, if we so choose (κατὰ προαίρεσιν)."[55]

Proairesis is also referred to as man's intention; our will to do the will of God; or man's free choice for God: "Nothing is impossible for this good intention and will. ... By correcting our will and intention we can correct the defects of our nature and overcome its infirmities. Thanks to his will, man who was previously fallen can now begin to follow the will of God. ... By its union with the desire for God ... our will becomes much stronger than it was before. ... It is not any will or any desire that brings about this change in man; it is the desire for God and love for Christ —a love that is nourished by grace."[56]

---

[54] *A Patristic Greek Lexicon*, ed. G. Lampe, p. 1133.

[55] St. Maximos, *Two Hundred Texts on Theology* 2. 84, PG 90, 1164C, trans. pp. 158-159. See St. Basil, "Virtue comes into being out of free choice (προαιρέσεως) and not out of constraint." *God Is Not the Cause of Evil* 7, PG 31, 345B, trans. N. Harrison, p. 75.

[56] Archbishop Demetrios, 'Man Fallen and Restored', *Sobornost* 4. 10. 1964, pp. 573-574.

We re-direct our free will away from self-centeredness by orienting our daily life toward Christ-likeness. The ascetic practices of our Church provide daily opportunities assisting us in this spiritual 're-orientation'. Fasting, prostrations, almsgiving, abstinence, obedience and self-restraint are not ends in themselves. These ascetic practices are means by which we are purified from our unnatural passions, and through which we acquire spiritual virtues and become like Christ.

Ultimately, ascetic practices are expressions of our freedom to choose God. Ascetic practices are not intended to appease God. Rather, they are spiritual therapy.

Ascesis is the Greek word for exercise. In Modern Greek, the word ἄσκησις refers to athletic exercises or military drills training soldiers for combat.[57] Ascetic practices such as fasting and prostrations are spiritual exercises. Just as we seek to develop and maintain physical, bodily health, we must do likewise for the spiritual health of our soul.

One of the basic ways we exercise and grow spiritually is through fasting. Through this small yet prayerful sacrifice we 'put off' the old man, who lives contrary to nature, and bring to life the new man, living foremost for Christ.

---

[57] *Oxford Greek-English Learner's Dictionary*, ed. D. Stavropoulos, Oxford, 1988, pp. 130-131.

Fasting is essential as we struggle to re-direct our spiritual lives toward Christ, Who Himself fasted forty days in the wilderness. Fasting is one of the basic steps in becoming like Christ.

When fasting, even in little ways, we exercise our freedom; our *true* freedom for self-control; our freedom to say no to self-centeredness; our freedom to focus not so much on ourselves but on God and on others. Fasting is essential for preparing before Holy Communion and the celebration of every major Church feast.

Fasting for its own sake is not the goal. Fasting is a means to an end. We fast in order to focus, to re-focus ourselves on communion with Christ. The Greek word for repentance (μετάνοια) means literally a change or re-focusing of our minds, hearts and entire life back to Christ.[58]

God gives us this great gift of freedom. We are free to embrace and follow Him, or remain indifferent and reject His Incarnation. It is up to us to decide freely.

In the divinely inspired Wisdom of Sirach, we read, "He Himself created man in the beginning and left him in the counsel of his will. If you will, you will keep the commandments, and faithfully do His good pleasure. He has set before you fire and water; if you will, stretch forth your hand, life and death are before mankind, and whichever he chooses, it will be given to him. For great is the wisdom of the Lord."[59]

---

[58] See John 14. 6.
[59] Wisdom of Sirach 15. 14-18 (SAAS).

Chapter Three: Panayia

Introduction

She was about 16 years old when she became pregnant.[1] The only child of aged parents, this young girl would alter the very destiny of the human race. The impact she left cannot be matched. Every generation calls her blessed.[2]

She is known as the most famous mother of all time and the most famous virgin. What a paradox! A virgin birth! A virgin mother! Who can imagine such a thing?

The Bible confirms the Virgin Birth of our Lord.[3] The belief Christ was born of a virgin has been upheld from apostolic times. In fact, affirming this might be our first step toward true faith, the initial 'mustard seed' of faith that can move mountains.[4]

Belief in the Virgin Birth is stated in the Nicene Creed, where we confess Christ is truly "Incarnate of the Holy Spirit and of the Virgin Mary, and became man."

---

[1] See *The Protoevangelium of James* 12.
[2] See Luke 1. 48.
[3] Luke 1. 27, 34.
[4] See Matt. 13. 31-32.

Belief in the Virgin Birth is not an option. It is a formal doctrine of the Christian faith. All the depth and beauty of our Orthodox Faith begins with this first step of child-like faith that a virgin gave birth to the Son of God.

Panayia as Mother

The motherhood of Panayia[5] is a great mystery. Throughout the earthly life of our Lord, and even now, there is one human being to whom He is most intimately connected. Christ enjoyed the same, yet unique relationship that every child shares with his or her own mother.[6]

The loving bond our Lord and God had, and continues to have, with His mother must be similar in human terms to our relationship with our mother: "Even an ordinary motherly love culminates in a spiritual identification with the child, which implies so often sacrifice and self-denial. Nothing less can be assumed in the case of Mary."[7]

She is recognized not only for giving birth to Christ, but for raising Him from His infancy. His mother remained near, not only from His birth and growth into manhood, but up until the very end of His earthly life.

---

[5] In Modern Greek, the name 'Panayia' (literally, 'All Holy') is a more prevalent, personal and intimate way of referring to or calling upon the Mother of God. The name 'Theotokos' ('Mother of God' or 'Birthgiver of God') is a more formal, official and theological title.
[6] See Florovsky, *Creation and Redemption*, Belmont, 1976, pp. 175-176.
[7] G. Florovsky, *Creation and Redemption*, p. 185.

Not only were His first words and glances, as an infant, directed toward His mother; but also His last, as His bloodied Body hung, nailed onto the Holy Cross.[8] From the moment of His miraculous conception, to His brutal Crucifixion, Panayia remained at the side of her beloved Son.

Fr. Florovsky writes: "Motherhood, in general, is by no means exhausted by the mere fact of a physical procreation. It would be lamentable blindness if we ignored its spiritual aspect. In fact, procreation itself establishes an intimate spiritual relation between the mother and the child. This relation is unique and reciprocal, and its essence is affection or love. Are we entitled to ignore this implication of the fact that our Lord was 'born of the Virgin Mary'?"[9]

Panayia was not just a tool or conduit through which God came into the world.[10] She is truly His mother. She is the Mother of God.

---

[8] See John 19. 26.

[9] Florovsky, *Creation and Redemption*, p. 175. He adds, "It would be impertinent indeed to intrude upon the sacred field of this unparalleled intimacy between the Mother and the divine Child. But it would be even more impertinent to ignore the mystery. In any case, it would have been a very impoverished idea if we regarded the Virgin Mother merely as a physical instrument of our Lord's taking flesh." Ibid., pp. 175-176.

[10] See St. John Damascene, *Exact Exposition* 3. 12.

The Ministry of Panayia to Mankind

One thing should be clear. There is only one Savior of mankind—and this is our Lord Jesus Christ. Yet Christ was not simply a prophet or exalted angel. Christ is the Only Begotten Son of God Who was truly born as man, born as the only son of a human mother. Although there is only one mediator between God and man—our Lord and Savior Jesus Christ—still, the ministry of Panayia must not be minimized.

Professor Mantzaridis explains, "The Blessed Virgin, who was made worthy to become the mother of Christ, also made possible His dwelling in every man. We receive Christ because of the Blessed Virgin who was made worthy to give birth to Him as man. Again, there remains one God and mediator between God and man, Christ. But this mediation became possible through the Blessed Virgin. Christ saves us as the Son of the Virgin. ... The Mother of God does not redeem us; the Mother of God is not God. But we cannot be redeemed without her; we do not become 'participants in the divine nature' (2 Peter 1. 4) without the Blessed Virgin."[11]

Panayia offered an unprecedented ministry to mankind. We cannot ignore her fundamental role in God's plan, not only for our salvation, but also for the sanctification of our human nature. Only with this teenage virgin's consent does God truly become man. She freely consented to give birth to God: "Let it be to me according to your word."[12]

---

[11] G. Mantzaridis, *Orthodox Spiritual Life*, trans. K. Schram, Brookline, 1994, pp. 97-98.
[12] Luke 1. 38.

With these few words, the young virgin initiates the fulfill-ment of God's supreme plan for mankind.[13]

It is important to note the Incarnation of God was not only the work of the Holy Spirit Who descended upon the Vir-gin. It was also the work of the will, faith and free consent of the young Virgin herself: "For, neither would it have been possible, had the Blessed Virgin not prepared herself ... for God to look kindly on mankind and to desire to de-scend to earth, that is, had there not been someone to re-ceive Him, someone capable of serving Him in the econ-omy of salvation; nor would it have been possible, had she not believed and given her consent for God's will for us to have been realized."[14]

Fr. Florovsky comments on the pivotal role of Panayia's free-will: "The Incarnation was indeed a sovereign act of God, but it was a revelation not only of his omnipotent might, but above all of his fatherly love and compassion. There was implied an appeal to human freedom once more ... Mary was voicing this obedient response of man to the redeeming decree of the divine love, and so she was rep-resentative of the whole race. She exemplified in her per-son, as it were, the whole of humanity."[15]

---

[13] "Her voice was a mighty voice ... and the Word of the Father was formed by the word of a mother, and the Creator is created by the voice of a creature. And just as when God said, 'Let there be light', 'at once there was light', so, as soon as the Virgin spoke, the true Light dawned; and He ... was joined to the flesh and carried in the womb. O sacred voice! O words of great power! O blessed tongue!" St. Nicholas Cabasilas, *Homily on the Annunciation* 10, trans. Orthodox Tradition 22. 2, 2005, p. 11.
[14] St. Nicholas Cabasilas, *Homily on the Annunciation* 4, p. 5.
[15] G. Florovsky, *Creation and Redemption*, p. 181.

To put it simply, Panayia is the purest and most precious human person mankind could have ever offered to God. All human history anticipated her appearance. All creation awaited her birth. She is the unique chosen one of God.

Panayia is the Mother of our Creator. She made Him a partaker of our human nature. She did not simply provide a body as the means through which God was born. She was not just any virgin. Panayia freely offered herself to the Creator in an unprecedented way.

Her heart burned with desire for God alone. Rejecting every sinful thought, she acquired every spiritual virtue. She alone enjoyed extraordinary peace with God. By her unparalleled spiritual beauty, Panayia attracted the gaze of our Creator toward herself: "Having trained both body and soul to receive such beauty, she turned the gaze of God towards herself, and by her own beauty rendered our common nature beautiful and won over the Impassible One."[16]

Regarding her unique spiritual stature, St. Nicholas Cabasilas adds: "It is clear that there was no point to which she had to progress ... neither was there anything that she had to add to what she already possessed, nor was it possible for her to become greater in virtue, since she had attained to the very pinnacle of sanctity. ... It was for this very reason that she came into existence ... she who ... trained her soul so well that she was preferred by God the Judge to all of humanity. ... He did not choose for His Mother the best of all those in existence, but her who was absolutely the best ...

---

[16] St. Nicholas Cabasilas, *Homily on the Annunciation* 2, p. 4.

"Nor did He choose her who was more suitable for Him than anyone else in the human race, but her who so totally suited Him."[17]

Panayia in Holy Tradition

Several Church Fathers contrast the 'two virgins' or 'two Eves'.[18] The first virgin, Eve, was disobedient toward God and became the cause of bodily and spiritual death for mankind. The second Eve, the Virgin Mary, was obedient to God and became the cause for true and eternal life: "Between the two Eves lies all the history of the Old Testament, the past from which she who has become the Mother of God cannot be divided."[19]

The period of the Old Testament was a time of waiting for the advent of Panayia. Her birth from the aged and barren Joachim and Anna initiates the passing away of the Old Testament. With the birth of Panayia, the time of Old Israel is fulfilled: "It is beyond any question that she who was chosen to be the Mother of God represents the summit of Old Testament holiness ... The All-Holy Mother of God belongs not only to the Old Testament, where she is hidden and does not appear, but also to the Church ... The most holy Virgin passes from the Old to the New; and this transition, in the person of the Mother of God, shows us how the New Covenant is the fulfillment of the Old."[20]

---

[17] St. Nicholas Cabasilas, *Homily on the Annunciation* 7 and 8, p. 9.
[18] E. g., St. Irenaeus, *Against Heresies* 5. 19. 1; St. Justin Martyr, *Dialogue with Trypho* 100; St. Jerome, *Letters* 22.
[19] Lossky, *In the Image and Likeness of God*, Crestwood, 1974, p. 203.
[20] Ibid., p. 201.

In the Old Testament, she is referred to in the prophecy of Isaiah: "Therefore the Lord Himself shall give you a sign; Behold, a virgin shall conceive and bear a son, and shall call His name Emmanuel."[21] In the New Testament, she is mentioned at various points throughout our Lord's life and ministry, especially with reference to His Birth and Death. Within the life of Holy Tradition, however, her veneration is widespread.[22]

The most important ancient writing that reveals the high respect reserved for Panayia is *The Protoevangelium of James* (also known as *The Gospel of James* or *The Book of James*). Likely composed in the mid-second century, *The Protoevangelium of James* records events primarily from the life of Panayia, rather than focusing specifically on the life of Christ. It is an important source that had wide impact on the life of Holy Tradition. Translated into a variety of languages, this writing greatly influenced the life of the early Church.

The Protoevangelium of James recounts the events surrounding the birth of Panayia, her dedication to the Temple at the age of three, her betrothal to Joseph, as well as the Annunciation and Birth of Christ. *The Protoevangelium* provides the names of her aged parents, Joachim and Anna, and also states Joseph was a widower with children of his own at the time Mary was entrusted to his care.[23]

---

[21] Isaiah 7. 14.

[22] "The mystery of the Mother of God was revealed only to those within the Church... More than an object of faith, this mystery is ... a fruit of faith, ripened in Tradition." Lossky, *In the Image and Likeness of God*, p. 209.

[23] See *The Protoevangelium of James* 9.

The Protoevangelium states that Sts. Joachim and Anna were a pious elderly couple unable to have children. They were extremely saddened for many years. After much heartfelt prayer, and miraculous intervention, St. Anna conceived.[24] They named their daughter Mary. Since they are the parents of Panayia, Sts. Joachim and Anna are the maternal grandparents of Christ.

Even though their names are not mentioned in the New Testament, Sts. Joachim and Anna are commemorated at the conclusion of many liturgical services, including the very end of every Divine Liturgy: "Through the prayers of Sts. Joachim and Anna ..."

According to St. Paisios of Mount Athos: "Saints Joachim and Anna were completely spiritual people, without any carnal-mindedness at all. They were the most passionless couple that has ever lived. First, they prayed to God separately, with tears, that He would give them a child, and then they came together, out of obedience to God and not out of any carnal desire. And, since the conception happened without self-indulgent pleasure, Panayia was all-pure and chaste. Of course, she wasn't free from ancestral sin, [as is upheld in the Roman Catholic doctrine of the Immaculate Conception], because she was conceived in the usual or natural way ... but still it was totally without passion, as God wanted people to be born."[25]

---

[24] See *The Protoevangelium of James* 1-5.
[25] Hiero. Isaac, *Elder Paisios of Mount Athos*, Ormylia, 2012, p. 144.

As stated in *The Protoevangelium*, when their daughter reached the age of three, Joachim and Anna fulfilled their vow to God. They dedicated Mary to a life of virginity within the Temple at Jerusalem. They brought her to the High Priest Zacharias, husband of Panayia's first cousin Elizabeth, who was waiting for her at the Temple's entrance.[26] There in the temple she lived and grew, from childhood into adolescence.[27]

From the earliest age, Panayia lived in the Temple, without any worldly cares, desires or concerns: "She lived for God alone, her intellect fixed at every moment on the contemplation of His beauty. During her sojourn in the Temple, the holy child, through continuous prayer and vigilance, accomplished the purification of her heart. ... She adorned herself as a bride in the splendid raiment of the virtues ..."[28]

---

[26] See *the Protoevangelium of James* 7. The Entry of the Most Holy Theotokos into the Temple (November 21) is a major feast of the Orthodox Church.

[27] In addition to prayer and the study of Holy Scripture, the young Panayia occupied herself with weaving, see Θρησκευτικὴ καὶ Ἠθικὴ Ἐγκυκλοπαιδεία, vol. 5, Athens, 1964, p. 452.

[28] *The Synaxarion* vol. 2, November 21, Ormylia, p. 194. See St. Gregory Palamas, *Homilies* 53. 47, ed. and trans. C. Veniamin, p. 435.

When she reached the age of adolescence, it was time for her to leave the Holy Temple.[29] According to *The Proto-evangelium*, the priests sought a suitable man who could be entrusted with the welfare of the young virgin. Lots were drawn and the elderly widower Joseph of Nazareth became the Betrothed of Panayia.[30] She was taken from the Temple and entrusted to the chaste Joseph, who vowed to guard her virginity.

St. Joseph the Betrothed played a prominent role during the infancy and childhood of Christ. Not only was he guardian of the newborn Christ during the Flight into Egypt,[31] he was also the Lord's provider from infancy to adolescence. Joseph also provided the Christ-Child with extended family of close-knit relatives.

During these formative years of childhood, it would have been Joseph's family, as well as relatives of Panayia's parents, Sts. Joachim and Anna, who would have surrounded the young Christ.[32]

---

[29] "Reaching marriageable age, she was taken from the sanctuary by the priests and elders, who feared lest the custom of women come upon her there." *The Synaxarion* vol. 2, Nov. 21, Ormylia, ibid., p. 194. *The Protoevangelium of James* 8 states she was 12 years old, not uncommon for marriage in some Eastern cultures at that time.
[30] See *The Protoevangelium of James* 9.
[31] Matt. 2. 13-15.
[32] E. g., Luke 2. 44.

Tradition teaches Joseph fathered seven children from his previous marriage, four sons and three daughters.[33] The names of his four sons were: James (Iakovos) whom the Orthodox Church commemorates as the Brother of our Lord (Ὁ Ἀδελφόθεος) on October 23, as well as Joses, Jude and Simon.[34]

These men would have been step-brothers of Christ. The names of Joseph's three daughters were Esther, Martha and Salome, step-sisters of Christ.

The person of Joseph, and his extended family, played an important role within the life of Christ. Many people from Mediterranean countries or the Near East are especially close-knit with extended relatives. Cousins and in-laws are often considered brothers and sisters. If there is any truth to the accounts from Holy Tradition, many of those mentioned in the Gospels, with important roles within the life and ministry of our Lord, were in fact related to Him.

For example, according to Tradition, Joseph's daughter Salome married Zebedee, with whom she had two sons: James and John (the Theologian).[35] This means St. John the Theologian would have been the grandson of St. Joseph and therefore a step-nephew of Christ. Christ and Salome (Joseph's daughter) were step-brother and sister, since legally they were both children of Joseph. In this way, Christ was a step-uncle of St. John the Theologian.[36]

---

[33] See *The Synaxarion* vol. 2, Dec. 26-31, Ormylia, p. 562.
[34] See Matt. 13. 55, 56.
[35] See Matt 4. 21.
[36] See *The Synaxarion* vol. 1, Sept. 26, Ormylia, p. 199.

Many uncles and nephews have close relationships. Holy Tradition teaches it was John who was the disciple 'whom Jesus loved' who leaned on His breast at the Last Supper.[37] As the Lord died upon the Holy Cross, He entrusted the care of His mother to "the disciple whom He loved."[38] Holy Tradition identifies John as the 'Beloved Disciple'.[39]

Further relatives of Christ are found on Panayia's side. This line of descent is associated with her mother, St. Anna, the grand-mother of Christ.[40] Christ grew up as a beloved son, uncle, nephew and cousin. Not only did the Son of God assume our human nature, He also experienced the same human relationships with His various relatives, just as any member of a Jewish family in His day.

Not only was His family obviously important to Him, but Christ promises to those who believe in Him they too can become His true kinsmen: "Then His brothers and His mother came, and standing outside they sent to Him, calling Him. And a multitude was sitting around Him; and they said to Him, 'Look, Your mother and Your brothers are outside seeking You'.

---

[37] John 13. 23-25.
[38] John 19. 26.
[39] See *The Synaxarion* vol. 1, Sept. 26, Ormylia, 1999, p. 199.
[40] According to Tradition, St. Anna was the daughter of the priest Matthas. In addition to Anna, he also had two other daughters, Maria and Sobea. Sobea had a daughter, Elizabeth, who married the priest Zacharias, and gave birth to St. John the Baptist (Luke 1. 13). If this is true, since Sobea and Anna were sisters, their daughters Elizabeth and Panayia would have been first cousins. This would mean that their sons, Christ and John the Baptist, were second cousins. See *The Synaxarion* vol. 6, July 25, Ormylia, p. 264.

But He answered them, saying, 'Who is My mother, or My brothers?' And He looked around in a circle at those who sat about Him, and said, 'Here are My mother and My brothers! For whoever does the will of God is My brother and My sister and mother."[41]

The Theotokos: A Theological Perspective

As the Mother of God, Panayia has a prominent place within Orthodox theology. Any theological discussion pertaining to Panayia relates directly to the Person of Christ. Belief in the Incarnation of God—that God became man in the person of Jesus Christ—requires that Panayia be the Birth-giver or Mother of God.

St. John Damascene writes, "The Son of God became incarnate and was born of her. ... How, then, is she not Mother of God who from herself brought forth God incarnate? Actually, she is really and truly Mother of God ... being accounted both handmaid and mother of the Creator."[42]

The title 'Theotokos' is seen in light of this Christological perspective. It summarizes our belief that Christ is truly God and truly human: "Christological doctrine can never be accurately and adequately stated unless a very definite teaching about the Mother of Christ has been included. ...

---

[41] Mark 3. 31-35. See Matt. 12. 46-50 and Luke 8. 19-21.
[42] St. John Damascene, *Exact Exposition* 4. 14, PG 94,1161A, trans. F. Chase, p. 365. See St. Gregory the Theologian, *Epistle* 101. 5, PG 37, 177C.

"In fact, all the ... doubts and errors [concerning Mary] of modern times depend on the last resort precisely upon an utter Christological confusion. They reveal a hopeless 'conflict in Christology'. There is no room for the Mother of God in a 'reduced Christology'. Protestant theologians simply have nothing to say about her. Yet to ignore the Mother means to misinterpret the Son. ... The Mystery of the Incarnation includes the Mother of the Incarnate."[43]

The title Theotokos is above all a Christological term expressing, in one word, the Orthodox Church's teaching on the full and complete divinity, as well as the full and complete humanity, of our Lord Jesus Christ: "Theotokos is more than a name or an honorific title. It is rather a doctrinal definition—in one word. It has been a touchstone of the true faith and a distinctive mark of Orthodoxy even before the Council of Ephesus (431)."[44] According to St. John Damascene, the name Theotokos "expresses the entire mystery of the Incarnation."[45]

It is interesting to compare how the person of Panayia is virtually non-existent for many Protestant denominations, both doctrinally as well as in terms of devotion. On the other hand, Roman Catholicism often over-states her role, for example, in statues depicting the Blessed Virgin Mary standing alone, apart from Christ.

---

[43] G. Florovsky, *Creation and Redemption*, pp. 172-173.
[44] G. Florovsky, *Creation and Redemption*, p. 171.
[45] St. John Damascene, *Exact Exposition* 3. 12, PG 94, 1029C, trans. F. Chase, p. 294.

In the Orthodox Church, as in our icons, Panayia always holds the Christ-child.[46] It is Christ Who commands our attention. For the Orthodox Church, Panayia has no theological, spiritual or liturgical relevance apart from Christ.

Roman Catholic Exaggerations

In Roman Catholicism, there is an over-exaggeration of the Virgin Mary.[47] A notable example is the Roman Catholic dogma of Mary's Immaculate Conception. This erroneous doctrine states Panayia was *not* born with the same fallen nature as all humanity. She was granted a special, extraordinary grace when *she* was conceived within her mother's womb. This places her outside our shared human nature. She is thus immune to mankind's common fallen condition. She is not one of us. For Roman Catholicism, this is what makes the Virgin Mary so uniquely venerable.[48]

---

[46] Rarely is she depicted alone.

[47] Regarding Roman Catholic theological teachings, see St. John Maximovitch, *The Orthodox Veneration of Mary the Birthgiver of God*, Platina, 1994, pp. 47-61.

[48] "The [Roman Catholic] dogma of the Immaculate Conception was proclaimed by ... Pope Pius IX in 1854. The definition of this dogma says that the Most Holy Virgin Mary at the moment of her conception was cleansed of ancestral sin. ... According to the Roman teaching ... the Most Holy Virgin Mary had been removed from the general law of the 'deprivation of grace' and of the guilt of the sin of Adam. ... She received, in the form of an exception, a supernatural *gift*, a grace of sanctity, even before her birth, that is, at her conception." Pomazansky, *Orthodox Dogmatic Theology*, Platina, 2005, pp. 193-194.

The Orthodox Church rejects the doctrine of the Immaculate Conception. St. John Maximovitch writes, "None of the ancient Holy Fathers say that God in miraculous fashion purified the Virgin Mary while yet in the womb; and many directly indicate that the Virgin Mary, just as all men, endured a battle with sinfulness, but was victorious over temptations and was saved by her Divine Son."[49]

Panayia was conceived in the same way as all of us. She was born in the same fallen condition we share in common: "She was without sin under the universal sovereignty of sin ... She was not placed above history in order to serve a special divine decree but realized her unique vocation while in the chains of history ..."[50]

Panayia also struggled with her own temptations but she overcame them, by God's grace, and the correct use of her free-will. For the Orthodox Church, this is what makes her so uniquely venerable. She is the perfect example of what man can attain through the synergy of divine grace and human freedom. She overcame every self-centered and sinful temptation that would have separated herself from the grace of God.

---

[49] St. John Maximovitch, *The Orthodox Veneration of Mary the Birthgiver of God*, trans. S. Rose, Platina, 1994, p. 51.
[50] V. Lossky, *In the Image and Likeness of God*, p. 204.

According to St. Silouan, "Never by a single thought did the Mother of God sin, nor did she ever lose grace, yet vast were her sorrows; when she stood at the foot of the Cross her grief was as boundless as the ocean."[51]

She is not exalted because she was given a supernatural grace at her conception *separating* her from us. Rather, we venerate Panayia precisely because she *is* one of us, personifying our true spiritual potential.[52]

We are not bound by sin. If we indeed struggle with our fallen inclinations and weakened will, we too can choose, with the aid of God's grace, not to give in to sinful temptations separating us from Him.

St. Maximos teaches, "For just as Christ in His manhood was sinless by nature both in flesh and in soul, so we too who believe in Him, and have clothed ourselves in Him through the Spirit, can be without sin in Him if we so choose."[53]

---

[51] Archim. Sophrony, *St. Silouan the Athonite*, p. 390. "As if no man had dared to commit even one single sin, but all had abided by the Divine commandments and were still occupying their ancient habitation, thus did she ever keep her mind inviolate ..." St. Nicholas Cabasilas, *Homily on the Annunciation* 3, p. 4.

[52] "It is not by virtue of a privilege received at the moment of her conception by her parents that we venerate the Mother of God more than any other created being. She was holy and pure from all sin from her mother's womb, but still this holiness does not place her outside the rest of humanity." Lossky, *In the Image and Likeness*, p. 203.

[53] St. Maximos, *Two Hundred Texts on Theology* 2. 84, PG 90, 1164C, trans. *The Philokalia* 2, pp. 158-159. See St. John Damascene, *Exact Exposition* 2. 12, PG 94, 924A, trans. F. Chase, p. 235.

Protestant Misconceptions

Most Protestant denominations ignore Panayia. There is no place for her in the Protestant experience of Christ. She is rarely depicted and discussed. For those who do not know Panayia as Mother of God, the focus is often on the Cross and the sacrificial Death of Jesus, rather than on Christ's regeneration and deification of human nature.

While upholding that Christ is the divine Son of God, many Protestant confessions do not fathom the spiritual significance, nor the full theological implications, of God becoming man. The broader effects of the Incarnation and its consequences for our human nature are rarely mentioned. The Protestant emphasis is often placed on our *individual* relationship with Jesus.

For Western Christianity, Jesus is often seen as a perfect human example, whom the believer is called to *imitate*. For Protestant confessions the emphasis is often focused on the human side, the human sacrifice and human psychology of Jesus, rather than the divine Person of Christ our God Almighty, Who truly became man, and in Whose divine life we are called to *participate*.

For Western denominations, salvation is sometimes minimized to being forgiven for sins so we can escape the torments of hell. Salvation is reduced to being acquitted by God the Supreme Judge—if only we accept His Son as our personal Savior. In these denominations, Panayia has little or no spiritual, theological or liturgical relevance, whatsoever.

The Orthodox Church, however, knows Christ as the Son of God—the glorious Creator and Lord of the Universe. Christ renews, resurrects and deifies human nature by personally uniting it to His divine nature. We are created to participate in divine life through personal participation in the ascetic, sacramental and liturgical life of Christ's Holy Body—His Holy Church.

The Virtue of Virginity

Any discussion of Panayia points not only to the person of Christ, but to the true spiritual potential of each one of us. She is the model of deified humanity and summit of Orthodox spiritual life. She refused, by God's grace, any and all sinful temptations and passions separating us from God. She exemplifies the acquisition of every spiritual virtue.

Panayia is the primary example of defeating sin and being freed from carnal passions. She is the ultimate example of 'synergy'—the co-operation of divine grace and human freedom. And of all virtues personified by Panayia, virginity characterizes her best.

The virtue of Panayia's virginity goes beyond her physical purity. For most Protestant's, she remained a virgin only until Jesus was born. Then, according to them, she and Joseph shared natural conjugal relations, evidenced in the Bible referring to 'the brothers of Jesus'.[54]

---

[54] See Matt. 12. 46; Luke 8. 19; Mark 3. 31.

This, of course, is rejected by the Orthodox Church. As already noted, Tradition teaches Joseph was an elderly widower with children of his own. The 'brothers of Jesus' in the Gospels are, in fact, our Lord's 'step-brothers'.

For the Orthodox Church, Panayia remained Ever-Virgin through her entire life. The idea she and Joseph shared conjugal relations after the mysterious and glorious birth of our Lord and God is unthinkable, even blasphemous. St. John Damascene emphasizes: "Hence, the Ever-Virgin remained a virgin even after giving birth and never had converse with a husband as long as she lived. ... How, indeed, would she have given birth to God and have known the miracle from the experience of subsequent events and then have allowed intercourse with a husband? Far be it! The thinking of such things is beyond the bounds of prudent thought, let alone the doing of them."[55]

The Church's belief in Panayia's Ever-Virginity is conveyed in her icons. In most, her face is surrounded by three small 'stars': one on her forehead, and two on her shoulders. Her ever-virginity was officially stated as early as 553 at the 5th Ecumenical Council of Constantinople.[56]

Panayia remained Ever-Virgin, in body, mind and soul, throughout her entire life.

---

[55] St. John Damascene, *Exact Exposition* 4. 14, PG 94, 1161BC, trans. F. Chase, pp. 365-366. See St. John Maximovitch, *The Orthodox Veneration of Mary the Birthgiver of God*, Platina, 1994, pp. 31-33.
[56] See Θρησκευτικὴ καὶ Ἠθικὴ Ἐγκυκλοπαιδεία, vol. 8, p. 212.

Panayia's unprecedented dignity as the Virgin Mother of God exceeds the bounds of bodily virginity. More significantly, the purity of virginity extends to her soul as well. True virginity embraces our entire spiritual orientation: "Virginity is not simply a bodily status or a physical feature ... Above all it is a spiritual and inner attitude, and apart from that a bodily status would be altogether meaningless. The title of Ever-Virgin means surely much more than merely a 'physiological' statement. It does not refer only to the Virgin Birth. It excludes first of all any 'erotic' involvement, any sensual and selfish desires or passions, any dissipation of the heart and mind. The bodily integrity ... is but an outward sign of the internal purity."[57]

Purity is not confined to the physical body; true purity flows from the heart. This inner purity allows us to experience the presence of God: "Blessed are the pure in heart, for they shall see God."[58] The virtues of virginity, chastity and purity encompass the whole person—the complete man—including one's heart, soul and mind.[59]

Purification from our passions allows us to seek communion with God. This is our natural inclination as human beings. Our obsessions with sex and sexual 'orientation' are in fact un-natural. We are not created simply as sexual beings. We are created to grow as spiritual beings.

---

[57] Florovsky, *Creation and Redemption*, pp. 184-185. See St. Gregory Palamas, "Perfect virginity of soul means keeping the mind free from all association with evil." *Homilies* 44. 3, trans. C. Veniamin, p. 118.
[58] Matt. 5. 8.
[59] See Matt. 22. 37.

Sexual promiscuity is not merely a matter of one's body, but also the heart: "But I say to you that whoever looks at a woman to lust for her has already committed adultery with her in his heart."[60]

Panayia preserved her purity not only in body, but also in her heart. She never entertained an evil or sinful thought that would have distanced her from God. Although she was tempted, her entire life was oriented to God alone.[61]

Conclusion

We might ask ourselves, 'What does all of this have to do with me'? What does Panayia's purity actually mean to us struggling to lead Orthodox spiritual lives in contemporary society?

Actually, all of this has a lot to do with us.

Our Lord calls us not to simply commemorate His Virgin Birth. Rather, he calls us to practice and personalize this same virtue of purity in our own hearts and daily lives. In Orthodox spiritual life, we are called to realize our full spiritual potential. God desires to unite and dwell within each one of us, in a most intimate and personal way.

---

[60] Matt 5. 28.

[61] "It was an undisturbed orientation of the whole personal life towards God, a complete self-dedication. ... Our Lady perhaps had her temptations too, but has overcome them in her steady faithfulness to God's calling." Florovsky, *Creation and Redemption*, pp. 184-185.

For the Orthodox Church, the mystery that took place in Panayia's virgin womb also takes place within the heart of every believer: "The divine Logos, who once for all was born in the flesh, always in His compassion desires to be born in spirit in those who desire Him. He becomes an infant and moulds Himself in them through the virtues. He reveals as much of Himself as He knows the recipient can accept."[62]

According to Professor Mantzaridis: "Through the sacraments of the Church, especially in Baptism, Chrismation and the Holy Eucharist, Christ himself comes and dwells in man. And so the birth of Christ, which happened but once from the Blessed Virgin, is mystically repeated in the heart of each of the faithful. ... The faithful person takes the place of the Blessed Virgin spiritually and offers himself so that Christ may be born and formed within his existence. This birth and growth of Christ within him is his own spiritual birth and growth. Therefore, the person of the Blessed Virgin in the Orthodox tradition constitutes the most perfect example of spiritual exaltation toward God."[63]

Christ calls every believer to become, each in our own way, a little theotokos.[64] Christ is born and grows within us as we struggle to free ourselves from our passions and sins. He comes to live within us as we strive to acquire spiritual virtues that make us Christ-like.

---

[62] St. Maximos, *Various Texts on Theology* 1. 8, PG 90, 1181A, trans. *The Philokalia* 2, pp. 165-166.
[63] G. Mantzaridis, *Orthodox Spiritual Life*, pp. 29-30.
[64] See Metro. Hierotheos, *The Twelve Feasts of the Lord*, p. 36.

Metropolitan Hierotheos adds, "Christ, who was once born in the flesh, always wants to be born in the spirit in those who wish it, and so He becomes an infant, forming Himself in them through the virtues. Spiritual conception and birth become perceptible by the fact that ... there cease to be desires to commit sin, passions are inactive in the person, he despises sin and constantly wishes to do the will of God. ... Then the person becomes a temple of the Holy Spirit. The Annunciation to the Theotokos is an annunciation to the human race. This universal feast should contribute to our personal feast, to our personal annunciation."[65]

Panayia's love and prayers have never left Christ's Holy Church. Panayia intercedes for us all, with a mother's boldness before Christ, that we too may become "a soul that gives birth to God ... 'a *theotokos* by grace'."[66]

---

[65] Metro. Hierotheos, *The Twelve Feasts of the Lord*, pp. 36-37. St. Gregory of Sinai elaborates, "People who have received grace are as if impregnated and with child by the Holy Spirit; but they may abort the divine seed through sinning or divorce themselves from God through intercourse with the enemy lurking within them. It is the turbulence of the passions that aborts grace, while the act of sinning deprives us of it altogether. A passion-loving and sin-loving soul, shorn of grace and divorced from God, is the haunt of passions—not to say demons—in this world and the next." *On Commandments and Doctrines* 12, trans. *The Philokalia* 4, p. 214.

[66] Archim. Vasileios, *The Saint: Archetype of Orthodoxy*, trans. Theokritoff, Montreal, 1997, p. 40. See St. Symeon the New Theologian, *Ethical Discourses* 1. 9, 10.

Elder Vasileios concludes: "There is conceived within you the personified light which illumines our thoughts. There enters into you a little leaven which leavens the whole lump. By grace you carry Christ as a babe in the womb. ... You do not speak, or move, or act without reference to this 'pregnancy'. You do not make sudden movements. You do not quarrel. You forgive everyone. You judge no one—you have no time or inclination or mission to do anything of that sort, so as not to miscarry the baby you have conceived. This is the grace given to the monk..."[67]

---

[67] Archim. Vasileios, *Monastic Life as True Marriage*, trans. E. Theokritoff, Montreal, 1996, p. 24.

Chapter Four:
In the Image and Likeness of God

*"Then God said, 'Let Us make man
in Our image, according to Our likeness'."*
The Book of Genesis

Christ—The Image of God

The Orthodox understanding of human nature is based primarily on verses from Genesis: "Then God said, 'Let Us make man in Our image (κατ' εἰκόνα), according to Our likeness' ... So God created man in His own image, in the image of God He created him."[1] Man is created according to the 'image' (ἡ εἰκών) of God.[2]

In the New Testament, the same Greek word for 'image' (ἡ εἰκών) is used in relation to Christ. Christ Himself is the image of God, as St. Paul teaches in his Epistle to the Colossians: "He is the image of the invisible God."[3]

While we are created *in* the image, or *according* to the image of God, Christ is *the* image, that is to say, the identical or natural image of God. There is a fundamental difference. Technically speaking, Christ is *the* image of God, while man is created *according* to the image of God, or precisely, according to the image of Christ.

---

[1] Gen. 1. 26, 27. The phrase 'κατ' εἰκόνα' may also be translated as 'according to the image'.
[2] ἡ εἰκών is also the term the Church uses for her holy icons.
[3] Col. 1. 15. See also 2 Cor. 4. 4.

St. John Damascene writes: "There are different kinds of images. First there is the natural image. ... The Son is the natural image of the Father, precisely similar to the Father in every way, except that He is begotten by the Father ... Therefore the first kind of image is the natural image. ... [Another] kind of image is made by God as an imitation of Himself: namely, man."[4]

Christ is the *natural* image of God, while man is created *according* to this image: "The distinction is clear that Christ constitutes the image of God and man the image of Christ; that is to say, that man is the image of the Image."[5] The Orthodox understanding of human nature is focused on the Person of Christ.

Christ is the model or 'Archetype' on which Adam is created. Referring to Christ as the 'new man' or the 'new Adam', St. Nicholas Cabasilas explains, "It was for the new man [Christ] that human nature was created at the beginning ... He Himself is the Archetype for those who are created. It was not the old Adam who was the model for the new, but the new Adam [Christ] for the old ... For those who have known him first, the old Adam is the archetype because of our fallen nature. ..."

---

[4] St. John Damascene, *On the Divine Images* 3. 18, 20, PG 94, 1337C-1340C, trans. D. Anderson, Crestwood, 1980, pp. 74-76.
[5] P. Nellas, *Deification in Christ*, trans. N. Russell, p. 24.

"But for Him who sees all things before they exist, the first Adam is the imitation of the second [Christ]. It was in accordance with His pattern and image that he [Adam] was formed."[6]

Human nature was not created for man alone. From its origin, human nature was created for the Incarnation. Human nature was created to be assumed by the Person of the Son of God.

Our dignity as human beings is based on Christ, Who is simultaneously the model *on* which we are created, and the ultimate goal *toward* which we naturally tend.[7] This teaching that human nature is created for the sake of the Incarnation of Christ is found in other patristic writings.[8]

St. Gregory Palamas writes: "God adorned human nature in this way because He was going to clothe Himself in it. He was to assume it from the blood of the Virgin, transform it into something better, and set it on high above all principality and power ..."[9]

---

[6] St. Nicholas Cabasilas, *The Life in Christ* 6. 12, PG 150, 680AB, trans. C. Cantanzaro, Crestwood, 1974, p. 190. He continues, "While the former Adam fell greatly short of perfection, the latter [Christ] was perfect in all respects and imparted perfection to men and adapted the whole human race to Himself. How then would the latter [Christ] not be the model of the former? We must, then, regard Christ as the Archetype and the former Adam as derived from Him." Ibid., PG 150, 680A-681D, p. 191.

[7] See P. Nellas, *Deification in Christ*, p. 33.

[8] See P. Nellas, *Deification in Christ*, pp. 227-237.

[9] St. Gregory Palamas, *Homilies* 26, p. 207.

St. Nicholas Cabasilas adds: "For God did not create humanity with one purpose in mind only to decide later on to use it for a different purpose ... He created mankind with this end in view, that, when He needed to be born, He might take from it a Mother. Having first established this need as a kind of standard, He then fashioned man in accordance with it."[10]

St. Maximos also teaches: "This [the Incarnation] is the blessed end for which all things were created. This is the preordained divine goal of the origin of beings, which we define as the preordained end for the sake of which all things exist. ... It was with a view to this end [the Incarnation of Christ] that God brought forth the essence of all beings."[11]

St. Nicodemos of the Holy Mountain elaborates further: "Do you see that God made man in His own image for this reason, that man might be able to accommodate the Archetype through the Incarnation? Therefore, God created man as a link between the intelligible and the sensible worlds and as a recapitulation and summary of all creatures for this purpose, that by being united with man He might be united with all creatures, and that everything in heaven and on earth might be recapitulated in Christ ... that Creator and creation might be one."[12]

---

[10] St. Nicholas Cabasilas, *Homily on the Annunciation* 8, pp. 9-10.
[11] St. Maximos the Confessor, *To Thalassios: On Various Questions* 60, trans. N. Russell, in *Deification in Christ*, p. 36; PG 90 621A.
[12] St. Nicodemos of the Holy Mountain, *An Apology on Our Lady Theotokos*, trans. ibid., pp. 230-231.

He summarizes, "From what has been said, then, anyone can conclude that unquestionably the mystery of the Incarnation had to take place, for the chief and supreme and essential reason that this mystery was the preordained will of God ..."[13]

According to these Fathers, human nature is created to be united to God in Christ.

This is a primary distinction: the distinction between Christ Who is the direct, identical or *natural* image of God; and man, who is created *according* to, or *in*, the image of Christ.[14]

There is, however, another important distinction also fundamental to the Orthodox understanding of human nature.

---

[13] St. Nicodemos of the Holy Mountain, *An Apology on Our Lady Theotokos*, trans. ibid., p. 237.

[14] "Let us give back to the Image that which is according to the image, recognizing our value, honoring the Archetype ..." St. Gregory the Theologian, *Orations* 1. 4, PG 35, 397B, trans. N. Harrison, p. 58.

The Distinction Between Image and Likeness

The precise meaning of the phrase 'in the image and likeness' has occupied the minds of many throughout the history of the Church. In the original Hebrew, the words 'image' and 'likeness' are essentially synonymous.[15] For the Church Fathers, however, image and likeness have a distinct meaning.

The image is that which is given to us at the moment of our creation. It is the common property of all human beings.[16] Likeness to God, however, is something we must struggle to attain. Image is the innate potential within man for attaining Christ-likeness, while likeness refers to its achievement or realization. Attaining to this likeness of Christ is the ultimate purpose of life, the fundamental goal of human existence.

Metropolitan Kallistos (Ware) describes the distinction between image and likeness: "The image is the initial endowment conferred on man at creation, the likeness is his final aim to be attained through the correct exercise of human freedom, aided always by God's grace. Image is to likeness as potentiality to realization, or as starting-point to end-point. The image is not self-sufficient but forward-looking, directed always to its fulfillment in the likeness.

---

[15] "Most modern commentators refuse to accept the distinction between the two terms, resting their case on the original Jewish text in which the parallel terms *tselem* and *themouth* are essentially synonymous." G. Mantzaridis, *The Deification of Man*, trans. L. Sherrard, Crestwood, 1984, p. 21.

[16] See ibid.

"Man ... is throughout his life on a journey from the image to the likeness."[17]

The image is our innate *potential* given by God to become like Him. Likeness is actually *achieving* that potential.

Elder Sophrony refers to this same distinction, "When it is God's good pleasure to unite with the human being, man perceives within himself the action of a Divine force which transfigures him and makes him no longer just potentially godlike—in the image of God—but actually godlike in likeness of being."[18]

We are not created in a state of completed perfection. We are, however, endowed with the freedom to choose, to either live in pursuit of achieving our full potential, or else to digress toward the desecration and defacement of our true dignity as an icon of Christ.

Only through the proper use of our God-given freedom can we cooperate with divine grace in restoring the image of Christ within us, and attain to likeness with Christ, for which we are created. In the Person of Christ, divine nature and human nature are forever united as one. God not only became man—man can also become divine.

---

[17] K. Ware, 'The Mystery of the Human Person', *Sobornost*, vol. 3, num. 1, 1981, p. 68.
[18] Archim. Sophrony, *Saint Silouan the Athonite*, p. 184. "Not only the image, but also the likeness is natural in man ... It is in man's very nature to be like God: it is in the image's very nature to achieve its perfection in the realization of the likeness." J. Larchet, *Therapy of Spiritual Illness*, vol. 1, trans. K. Sprecher, Montreal, 2012, p. 18.

Man's spiritual perfection as he grows from the image to
the likeness of God is not simply sanctification, or deification. It is *Christ*-ification.[19] It is attaining to the likeness
of Christ.

The Image of God in Human Nature

In spite that our nature is now fallen and marred by sin
and separation from God, we still retain the divine image
in which we are created. The image of God in fallen man
is disfigured and distorted, but it has not been entirely destroyed or annihilated. Never are we totally deprived of
the divine image in which we are created.[20]

The image of God in man is not limited to one specific
quality or characteristic of human nature. Rather, it ema-
nates as "through a prism, throughout the whole of human
existence."[21]

Many Orthodox writers discuss various aspects or attributes of the image of God in man. Even within the writings of one particular author, the phrase 'in the image' may
take on a variety of connotations.[22] Some definitions vary,
due to the specific context the author was addressing.

---

[19] See P. Nellas, *Deification in Christ*, p. 24.
[20] "After our forefather's transgression in paradise through the tree,
we suffered the death of our soul—which is the separation of the soul
from God—prior to our bodily death; yet although we cast away our
divine likeness, we did not lose our divine image." St. Gregory Palamas, *Natural Chapters* 39, PG 150, 1148, trans. p. 363.
[21] G. Mantzaridis, *The Deification of Man*, p. 16.
[22] See ibid.

"Sometimes the expression 'in the image' refers to man's free will, or to his rational faculty ... sometimes to the soul along with the body, sometimes to the mind ... and sometimes comprehensively to the whole man."[23] For the most part, however, the divine image pertains primarily to the human soul.[24]

Soul

Generally speaking, in a secular sense, a soul is defined as "the principle of life, thought, or action in man or animals; the spiritual part of man in contrast to the purely physical; an entity distinct from the body; or, the seat of the emotions, feelings or sentiments; the emotional part of man's nature."[25]

This dictionary definition makes no mention, however, of our soul's unique value, which should be a foremost consideration: "There is nothing equal in value to the soul. ... the soul by itself is far more valuable than the whole world and any worldly kingdom ..."[26]

---

[23] P. Nellas, *Deification in Christ*, p. 22.

[24] See Met. Hierotheos, *Orthodox Psychotherapy*, trans. E. Williams, Levadia, 1994, p. 104. See also St. Gregory the Theologian, *Orations* 45. 7; PG 36, 632A and St. Gregory Palamas, *Natural Chapters* 40, PG 150, 1148CD.

[25] *Oxford English Dictionary*, 2nd ed., vol. 16, Oxford, 1989, p. 40.

[26] St. Macarios of Egypt, *The Freedom of the Intellect* 148, trans. *The Philokalia* 3, p. 352. See Matt. 16. 26.

St. Gregory Palamas emphasizes the unique abilities of the human soul, "The human soul is something great and wondrous, superior to the entire world; it overlooks the universe and has all things in its care; it is capable of knowing and receiving God, and more than anything else has the capacity of manifesting the sublime magnificence of the Master-Craftsman."[27]

St. John Damascene provides a more succinct definition: "A soul is a living substance, simple and incorporeal, of its own nature invisible to bodily eyes, activating an organic body in which it is able to cause life."[28]

Concerning the relationship between our soul and body, St. John Damascene also teaches, "The soul is united with the body, the entire soul with the entire body and not part for part. And it [the soul] is not contained by the body, but rather contains it, just as heat does iron ..."[29]

---

[27] St. Gregory Palamas, *Natural Chapters* 24, PG 150,1137A, p.356.
[28] St. John Damascene, *Exact Exposition* 2. 12, PG 94, 924B, p. 236.
[29] St. John Damascene, *Exact Exposition* 1. 13, PG 94, 853A, p. 198. See St. Gregory Palamas, "The soul, since it sustains the body with which it is created, is everywhere in the body, although not in the sense of being located in a place or encompassed; but itself sustains, encompasses and quickens the body ..." *Natural Chapters* 61,PG 150, 1165A, trans. *The Philokalia* 4, p. 374. "The soul is not held by the body but holds the body. It is not within the body as in a vessel or bag, but rather the body is within the soul." Met. Hierotheos, *Orthodox Psychotherapy*, trans. E. Williams, Levadia, 1994, p. 111. See also St. Gregory of Nyssa, *On the Soul*, PG 45, 217B.

Met. Hierotheos emphasizes that our soul and body come into existence together. The soul is created with the body at conception: "The embryo is endowed with a soul at conception. The soul is created at conception and the soul at that time is just as active as the flesh. As the body grows so the soul increasingly manifests its energies."[30]

Furthermore, St. Gregory Palamas teaches that our soul possesses a life of its own, distinct from our body. And every human soul will continue to exist, even when the body dies and decays: "The soul has life not only as an activity but also as its essence, since it is self-existent; for it possesses a spiritual and noetic life that is evidently different from the body's and from what is actuated by the body. Hence when the body dissolves, the human soul does not perish with it."[31]

The soul of an animal, however, does not have life 'in itself', like a human soul does. Rather, Palamas continues, the soul of an animal has life only as 'activity', that is to say, only when it animates a particular physical body.

---

[30] Metro. Hierotheos, *Orthodox Psychotherapy*, p. 108. See St. John Damascene, "The body and the soul were formed at the same time— not one before and the other afterwards ..." *Exact Exposition* 2. 12, PG 94, 921A, trans. p. 235.

[31] St. Gregory Palamas, *Natural Chapters* 32, PG 150, 1141B, p. 359.

"The soul of each animal not imbued with intelligence ... does not possess life as essence, but as activity ... the soul of animals consists of nothing except that which is actuated by the body. Thus, when the body dissolves, the soul [of animals] inevitably dissolves as well."[32]

In regard to the human soul, the Church Fathers delineate various aspects or attributes that reflect particular distinctions within it, without any sense of separation into isolated components or parts.[33]

These distinctions or attributes within the human soul are referred to by different names, some stemming from Greek philosophy: "St. Gregory Palamas teaches that as God is Nous, Word and Spirit, so also the soul has nous, word and spirit. ... Beyond these divisions St. Gregory ... also uses the division of the soul established at the time of the ancient Greek philosophers. Man's soul is one, although it has many powers. It is divided into three parts: the intelligence, the appetitive power and the incensive power."[34]

Among the various faculties or functions of the human soul referred to by the Church Fathers, we will focus on two aspects in particular—the nous and logos.

---

[32] St. Gregory Palamas, *Natural Chapters* 31, PG 150, 1141A, p. 359.
[33] See Metro. Hierotheos, *Orthodox Psychotherapy*, p. 111.
[34] Ibid., p. 247. For basic definitions of the intelligent, incensive and appetitive aspects of the soul, see *The Philokalia* vol. 1, London, p. 358.

Nous

The human soul is endowed with two particular attributes uniquely reflecting the divine image: the *nous* (ὁ νοῦς) and the *logos* (ὁ λόγος) or intelligence.[35] These two faculties are of primary importance. The nous and logos are linked together, yet not identical. Even though directly related, they remain distinct.

Our nous or noetic faculty uniquely attests to our being made in the image of God.[36] The term nous is unfamiliar to contemporary Western man, yet it is fundamental to Orthodox theology. It is a basic concept distinguishing the spiritual experience of the Orthodox East from all Christian denominations.

The English words 'mind' or 'intellect' are at times used to translate νοῦς, but they do not reflect the depth of its meaning.[37] Interestingly, the term nous is found in some English dictionaries, but its definition is opposite to patristic writings. This points to the underlying issue. Nous is often defined as 'reason, mind, intellect, or intelligent principle'.[38] For the Fathers of the Church, however, such a definition applies more to logos and not nous.

---

[35] See St. Gregory of Nyssa, *On the Making of Man* 5, PG 44, 137B.

[36] See St. Gregory Palamas, *Natural Chapters* 27 and 37, PG 150, 1137D and 1145B, trans. *The Philokalia* 4, pp. 357 and 362.

[37] The English translation of *The Philokalia* vols. 1-4, (Faber and Faber: London, 1979-1995) uses the word 'intellect' for νοῦς (nous).

[38] See *Webster's Third New International Dictionary*, ed. P. Gove, Springfield, 2002, p. 1546.

It is difficult to provide a comprehensive patristic definition for nous: "The term nous has many meanings in the
works of the Fathers. Sometimes it is identified with the
soul, sometimes it is an energy of the soul, or the eye of
the soul, sometimes the term suggests the essence of the
soul ..."[39]

St. John Damascene offers a straightforward definition,
"It [the soul] does not have the [nous] as something distinct from itself, but as its purest part, for, as the eye is to
the body, so is the [nous] to the soul."[40] These are more
preferable definitions of nous: 'the purest part of the soul',
or 'the eye of the soul'.

For the most part, Western man hasn't heard of the term
'nous'. Most of us are unaware of the presence of our own
nous. Contemporary man lives primarily through his intelligence. An over-reliance is placed on the role of intelligence, to the point where it can become detrimental to
one's spiritual life.[41]

---

[39] Metro. Hierotheos, *Orthodox Psychotherapy*, p. 125.
[40] St. John Damascene, *Exact Exposition* 2. 12, PG 94, 924B, p. 236.
[41] See Metro. Hierotheos, *Orthodox Psychotherapy*, pp. 206-214.

Logos

Logos (ὁ λόγος) is the Greek term for both 'word' and 'reason'. Logos is defined as "the word by which an inward thought is expressed; that which is said or spoken, a word or language" or "reason itself."[42] Logos is also translated as 'intelligence'.[43] We are intelligent and rational beings, gifted with the ability to speak with words in the logic of language, because we are created in the image of the Word of God.

The distinction between *nous* and *logos* is important: "The nous is that which see things clearly and therefore should be purified, and the intelligence [logos] is that which formulates and expresses what has been seen."[44] St. Maximos writes, "A pure [nous] sees things correctly. A trained intelligence [logos] puts them in order."[45]

We experience authentic spiritual life through the purification of our nous: "The nous has a relationship with God, it receives the energies of God; God reveals Himself to the nous, while intelligence ... is that which formulates and expresses the experience of the nous."[46]

---

[42] *A Greek English Lexicon*, ed. Liddell and Scott, Oxford, 1979, pp. 416-417.

[43] E. g., Mantzaridis, *The Deification of Man*, pp. 18-19 and Metro. Hierotheos, *Orthodox Psychotherapy*, p. 123.

[44] Metro. Hierotheos, *Orthodox Psychotherapy*, p. 123. "The [logos] of man is that which reveals what the nous perceives and experiences." Ibid., p. 204.

[45] St. Maximos, *Texts on Love* 2. 97, PG 90, 1016D, p. 82.

[46] Metro. Hierotheos, *Orthodox Psychotherapy*, p. 107.

After the Fall, our nous became dysfunctional. Our nous is now darkened and scattered. It is focused more on carnal passions and material possessions than on God. Our fallen intelligence now predominates, and it is also misdirected. We remain intelligent and retain our faculty of rational thought and speech. Yet we turn these away from God, and often against Him.

We become truly intelligent (λογικός) when our nous and logos are directed toward their natural goal, which is participation in the divine life of *the* Logos—Jesus Christ. Outside this environment, even though our intelligence remains, it too is fallen, darkened, and now functions separately from God: "After the Fall ... the intelligence was raised above the nous and now holds sway in fallen man. In fact this is the sickness of the ... intelligence. The intelligence is over-nourished, it has been raised to a greater position than the nous ... The over-nourished intelligence is the source of great abnormality in the spiritual organism. Arrogance, with all the energies of egoism, which is the source of the abnormality, is raging there."[47]

Arrogant intelligence is a characteristic mark of fallen humanity.

Throughout the history of the Church, many heretical leaders based their theological teachings on their own rational intelligence and intellectual abilities, rather than personal experience of God's grace and glory. These heretical teachers raised reason above revelation.

---

[47] Metro. Hierotheos, *Orthodox Psychotherapy*, pp. 206-207.

Metro. Hierotheos writes, "When human intelligence has dominion in a man, it leads him to a variety of heretical theories. Here the difference between philosophers and theologians is evident. The former philosophize about God. The latter, after purifying their nous, behold God. The former have a darkened nous and interpret everything one-sidedly through intelligence, while the Holy Fathers, the real theologians, acquire experience of God through their nous; and then intelligence serves their nous by expressing this inner experience in propositions."[48]

Elder Sophrony describes the dangers of over-inflated intelligence: "Intelligence...is by nature only one of the manifestations of life in the human personality ... Where it is allotted priority in the spiritual being of man, it begins to fight against its source—that is, its personal origin. ... When man's spiritual being is concentrated on and in the mind, reason takes over and he becomes blind to anything that surpasses him and ends by seeing himself as the divine principle."[49]

For many, it is easier to identify with our intelligence than with our nous. Most of us don't even know we have a nous. We are not aware of this higher aspect of our soul, something more important than intelligence. We are blind to the inner eye of our heart and soul.[50]

---

[48] Metro. Hierotheos, *Orthodox Psychotherapy*, p. 210.
[49] Arch. Sophrony, *St. Silouan the Athonite*, p. 165.
[50] "The whole of civilization is a civilization of the loss of the heart. ... The heart has died, the nous has been darkened, and we cannot perceive their presence." Met. Hierotheos, *Orthodox Psychotherapy*, p. 125.

In our fallen condition, we give intelligence a dispropor-
tionate role in our relationships with other people, and
with God. Contemporary man is held captive by the 'reign
of reason' imprisoning the Western world. As Orthodox
Christians, we must utilize our intelligence in the proper
way: "The nous receives grace ... and then sheds grace on
the intelligence as well. In this way intelligence becomes
a servant of the nous that is favored with grace, and we
return to our natural state. Intelligence which is not sub-
jected to this nous ... is sick and creates innumerable anom-
alies in our life, while, when it is subject to the nous it is
healthy and natural. This is the aim of the ascetic therapeutic training of the Church."[51]

Dominion

Our nous and logos are directly linked to other aspects
reflecting the image of God, for example, our dominion
over God's creation. Our intelligence and ability to think
logically afford us a predominance and sovereign role o-
ver creation. We have a unique ability to utilize the laws
of nature to our advantage.

However, our 'authority' is not contingent on intelligence
alone: "Our being in the image, and hence our kingly authority, is clearly not a matter of excelling other creatures
in certain natural properties (e. g., rational thought). It depends on the fact that God has given us certain properties
of His own."[52]

---

[51] Met. Hierotheos, *Orthodox Psychotherapy*, p. 214. For further reading, see ibid., pp. 214-337.
[52] E. Theokritoff, *Living in God's Creation,* pp. 70-71.

Our capacity to serve as steward and lord over all God's creation is another way in which the divine image is reflected in human nature.[53] This capacity to rule or govern is innate in us.[54] This calling to serve as the lord and master of God's creation must be seen in its proper perspective: "Man's 'oversight' of creation is not just practical management or 'stewardship'; it is inextricably bound up with being aware of the *mystery* of creation, discerning God's wisdom in the depths of created things."[55]

We are not meant to be a mere manager, but rather the mediator between God and His creation—the one who prayerfully offers creation back to our Creator through thankfulness, worship and praise. We are the agents through whom creation is offered back to its Creator.[56]

The fact that we are created with both a physical body and an immaterial soul gives us our exalted position within all creation. According to St. Gregory Palamas, "Man is created more perfectly in God's image than the angels, both because he possesses in himself a sustaining and quickening power and because he has a capacity for sovereignty. ... Angels do not have a body joined to them and subject to their [nous] ..."[57]

---

[53] See St. Gregory of Nyssa, *On the Making of Man* 4, PG 44, 136BC.
[54] See Genesis 1. 28.
[55] E. Theokritoff, *Living in God's Creation*, p. 68.
[56] See E. Theokritoff, *Living in God's Creation*, p. 214.
[57] St. Gregory Palamas, *Natural Chapters* 62, PG 150, 1165AB, trans. *The Philokalia* 4, pp. 374-375.

Our dominion over God's creation is shown in Adam's unique privilege of naming the animals, "God formed out of the ground all the wild animals of the field and all the birds of heaven, and brought them to Adam to see what he would call them. Thus whatever Adam called each living creature, that was its name."[58]

Our dominion as 'master' and 'lord' of all the creatures of the earth refers primarily to our relationship with creation *before* the Fall. This is to say, it refers to *pre*-fallen Adam: "Human dominion over other creatures was not revoked at the fall, but it was seriously modified. By no stretch of the imagination can we look at present relationships between man and other creatures and presume to read off God's original intention."[59]

---

[58] Genesis 2. 19.

[59] E. Theokritoff, *Living in God's Creation,* p. 73. She adds, "Man retains the degree of control necessary for his survival; but the natural authority flowing from the divine image has gone, to be replaced by a balance of terror. Depending on the species, either animals fear us, or we fear them." Ibid.

Love

Love is another attribute of human nature reflecting the image of God. Love is innate in us. It is essential to our very being.[60] Without love, the divine image is impaired and incomplete.[61]

For Orthodox theology, the entire teaching of the New Testament can be summed up in these three simple words: God is love.[62] God is love—and man is called to become like God through the practice of love, by giving love and receiving love. Man is created to live in love.

God is love. The more we love, the more we participate in divine life. It is through love that we attain to divine likeness and realize our true personhood. Love makes us truly human. Love makes us divine.[63]

---

[60] "The love of God is not something that is taught ... nor has anyone taught us to love our parents ... we have possessed the innate power of loving from the first moment of our creation." St. Basil, *Long Rules* 2, PG 31, 912A, trans. M. Wagner, Washington DC, 1962, pp. 233-234.
[61] See St. Gregory of Nyssa, *On the Making of Man* 5, PG 44, 137C.
[62] 1 John 4. 16.
[63] "The more perfect the love, the holier the life." *Saint Silouan the Athonite*, p. 366. Theoliptos of Philadelphia uses the term 'deifying love' (ἡ θεοποιὸς ἀγάπη), *On Inner Work in Christ*, PG 143, 381C, trans. *The Philokalia* 4, p. 177.

Without love, we distort the divine image in which we are created. The less we love, the more we alienate ourselves from divine life. Dostoevsky defines hell as "the suffering of being no longer able to love."[64]

Christ's commandments of love, to 'love your neighbor as yourself' and to 'love your enemies', reflect our underlying nature. The commandments of Christ manifest the truth that love is the way of God, and indeed the way toward God: "By this all will know that you are My disciples, if you have love for one another."[65]

Love for our neighbor leads to likeness with Christ.[66] On the other hand, without love for our fellow man, life loses its proper orientation: "Those who dislike and reject their fellow-man are impoverished in their being."[67] There is an obvious lack of love in our world today. This has great social ramifications.

At the same time, so many are out looking for love; yet often times, in the wrong places. All too often, we settle for the wrong kind of love. We settle for the wrong kind of relationships. We sometimes settle for relationships unlikely to contribute to our spiritual health.

---

[64] F. Dostoevsky, *The Brothers Karamazov* 2. 6. 3, trans. R. Pevear and L. Volokhonsky, New York, 1990, p. 322.

[65] John 13. 35.

[66] See St. Maximos, "Do not disdain the commandment to love, because by it you will be a son of God." *Texts on Love* 4. 20, PG 90, 1052C, trans. G. Berthold, New York, 1985, p. 77.

[67] Archim. Sophrony, *Saint Silouan the Athonite*, p. 116.

Even though we are fallen, there is something in our nature still hungering for love. There is something within us that still longs for the likeness of God.

Elder Sophrony comments on the fundamental role of love within our lives as human beings: "The commandment calls upon us to 'love'. It follows, therefore, that love is not something already given to us. Love must be acquired by the ascetic act of our free will. ... There is no more difficult, more painful spiritual endeavor than the struggle for the triumph of the love of Christ, first in ourselves, then in the whole world. In point of fact this love is not of the earth but of Heaven. In it lies the meaning of the Being of God Himself, Who is Love; Who gave us the commandment to love."[68]

Communion

God is three Persons—the Father, Son and Holy Spirit—Who share one nature and live in perfect love. God is love. In order to love, there must also be someone to be loved. At least two persons are needed for love. Love requires communion with another person or persons: "We cannot conceive of the person if there is no communion. The person does not live alone; he has reference, relationship, communion."[69] Man is created to live in loving communion with other persons.

---

[68] Archim. Sophrony, *We Shall See Him as He Is*, trans. R. Edmonds, Essex, 1988, p. 177.
[69] Metro. Hierotheos, *The Person in the Orthodox Tradition*, p. 213.

Communion in love is fundamental to our lives. This is seen in the basic unit of society, the family, where we first experience life as new-born infants. This is seen in the basic unit of the Church, the local parish, where we strive for fellowship with one another in a communion of love. This is seen in Orthodox monasticism, where a sisterhood or brotherhood struggles to share everything in common, including meals, possessions and in a very real way, their daily lives.

We are created to share our selves, our lives, our time, our personhood. Only in this way do we become truly human. Only in this way do we become like God.

We become Christ-like by emptying and sacrificing ourselves for other people. And until we sacrifice and share ourselves, and actually live for others, we remain as individuals, living in division among each other.

Man is created to share, not only in the lives of others, but also in the divine life of God. We were made to participate in God's eternal life of love and personal communion: "Man is not an autonomous and self-sufficient being ... communion and participation in divine life and glory is for man, his natural element."[70]

---

[70] J. Meyendorff, *Living Tradition*, Crestwood, 1978, p. 175.

Prayer for All Mankind

In our fallen state, we are not truly living as genuine human 'persons'. As each divine Person of the Holy Trinity contains the fullness of divine nature in His own unique Person, in a similar way, every human person is called to fulfill his true personhood by embracing all mankind within his own heart.[71]

To become a genuine human person, man must struggle to empty himself so that all mankind—every other human person—may be integrated within his own being, within his own heart. St. Paisios shares his personal experience, "For one to hold the entire world in his heart, he must broaden his heart. ... I feel such a tremendous maternal love, such an affection and tenderness, that I did not have before. The whole world can fit in my heart. I want to embrace all the people and help them. You see, love cannot remain closed up in the heart. Just like a mothers' milk needs to flow out when her child has died, love also needs to be released and given."[72]

---

[71] See Archim. Sophrony, *Saint Silouan the Athonite*, p. 122. Metropolitan Hierotheos warns that all analogies linked to the uncreated Holy Trinity, though useful and effective, are bound by limitations; see *The Person in the Orthodox Tradition*, p. 224.
[72] St. Paisios of Mount Athos, *Passions and Virtues*, pp. 217, 219.

When man, through prayer, descends into the depths of his heart, he "sees that the existence of mankind is not something alien and extraneous to him, but is inextricably bound up with his own being ... Through Christ's love all men become an inseparable part of our own individual, eternal existence."[73]

God has not only created us and given us life, but He has given us His very own divine life. He allows us to personally participate in His life of divine love. This Christ-like love embraces all mankind. Such all-embracing love, for every human person, is attained only *through* Christ and *in* Christ.[74]

To love all mankind is to pray for all mankind, as if one were praying for his own salvation: "All my desire is to learn humility and the love of Christ, that I may ... pray for all as I *pray for myself*,"[75] wrote St. Silouan.

---

[73] Archim. Sophrony, *Saint Silouan the Athonite*, p. 47.

[74] "[Christ] assimilates every man's existence and includes it in His own personal existence. The Son of man has taken into himself all mankind—He has accepted the 'whole Adam' and suffered for him." Ibid., p. 47.

[75] Ibid., p. 350. He adds, "I want only one thing: to pray for all men as for myself." Ibid. p. 102.

No one is saved alone.[76] No one who truly lives in Christ can remain disinterested or detached from the destiny of another human person; to do so is inconceivable because it contradicts the inherent unity of all mankind.[77]

Christ-like love leads naturally to Christ-like prayer for the salvation of all. This is the ultimate manifestation of the life in Christ. This is what it means to be alive in Christ; it is to acquire the same consciousness as Christ, the same compassion as Christ and the same desire that Christ has for the salvation of all.[78] Pure love, by nature, encompasses all mankind. And pure prayer strives for the salvation of every human being.[79]

Such prayer leads the believer to personally experience the ontological unity of all mankind. It leads to the awareness of mankind as a community of persons sharing the same nature.

---

[76] "Salvation ... means communion; and so there can be no disjunction of any kind between our personal salvation and the salvation of the world. The two form a unity. Our own salvation is necessarily linked to the salvation of every other human being ..." Met. Kallistos (Ware), "'We Must Pray for All': Salvation According to St. Silouan" in *Sobornost*, 19. 1, 1997, p. 54.

[77] "In spirit we translate our own individual state to universal dimensions. ... our spiritual merging with the world becomes a tangible reality." Arch. Sophrony, *On Prayer*, trans. Edmonds, Essex, 1996, p. 17.

[78] See 1 Tim. 2. 4.

[79] "When this spirit of Christ-like love enters within us, our soul thirsts for the salvation of all people." Archim. Sophrony, *We Shall See Him as He Is*, p. 202. For further reading on prayer for the salvation of all mankind in the teaching of St. Silouan and Elder Sophrony, see H. Boosalis, *Orthodox Spiritual Life According to St. Silouan the Athonite*, South Canaan, 2000, pp. 179-193.

"Through prayer [the Christian] integrates everyone into his own eternal life, whatever the geographical distance or historical time between them ... then no man is alien to him—he loves each and everyone, as Christ commands."[80]

Prayer for the salvation of all mankind is the manifestation of man's conformity to the divine image and likeness. It is personal participation in the communion of divine love. It is the realization of the divine potential inherent in man. Through Christ-like love for all mankind, man passes from mere individuality into genuine personhood.[81]

When limiting our lives within our individual nature, we fail to comprehend what it means to be human. We isolate ourselves, not only from each other, but also from God. Without Christ-like love for all people, our entire way of life becomes distorted. We become less than human; less than a true 'person' created in the image of God.

Such was the experience of the French existentialist philosopher Jean Paul Sartre: "Hell is other people."[82]

---

[80] Archim. Sophrony, *Saint Silouan the Athonite,* pp. 233-234.
[81] For further reading see Archim. Sophrony, *We Shall See Him as He Is,* pp. 190-235.
[82] See J. Sartre, "L'enfer, c'est les autres." *In Camera,* end of scene 5.

Conclusion: The Paradox of Human Perfection

Before concluding, there is one further point to mention. Our growth in Christ never really ends. We will never arrive at our final destination. The life in Christ, and our growth in Him, knows no limits. We are created with an innate capacity to continually grow spiritually, not only in this life, but also forever, throughout all eternity.

St. Gregory of Nyssa writes of man's eternal progress, "In the eternity of the age without end, he who runs towards Thee is always becoming greater and higher, always adding to himself by the multiplication of more exalted blessings. And he who ascends never ceases to go from beginning to beginning by beginnings which have no end."[83]

St. John Climacus adds: "Love has no boundary, and both in the present and in the future age we will never cease to progress in it ... even the angels make progress and indeed they add glory to glory and knowledge to knowledge."[84]

---

[83] St. Gregory of Nyssa, *On the Song of Songs* 8, PG 44, 941BC, trans. *The Synaxarion* vol. 3, Ormylia, 2001, p. 105. See *The Life of Moses* 1. 8, PG 44, 301B, trans. Malherbe and Ferguson, New York, 1978, p. 31.
[84] St. John Climacus, *The Ladder of Divine Ascent* 26, PG 88, 1068B, trans. Luibheid and Russell, p. 251.

Met. Kallistos explains, "Since God is infinite ... redeemed humanity will never cease to participate more and more fully in God's boundless glory and love. Our knowledge of him, while constantly increasing, will never be exhausted. The essence of perfection consists paradoxically in the fact that we never become perfect, but continue always to advance from 'glory to glory'. ... Eternity ... is not a closed circle but an upward-sloping line; it is not a geometrical point but an ever-ascending spiral."[85]

We don't achieve spiritual perfection in the sense of attaining a static state where we cease to advance. Perfection is not breaking through a barrier and arriving at spiritual completion. Divine life and love are infinite and eternal. We are made in the divine image, created to grow spiritually forever. We will never stop becoming more and more Christ-like—not only on earth but in heaven.

No matter what level of spiritual progress we reach, nor how many virtues we acquire, there always awaits us further growth—throughout all eternity.

Human nature is properly seen only in its original theological context: "Having been made in the image of God, man has a theological structure. And to be a true man he must at every moment exist and live theocentrically. When he denies God, he denies himself and destroys himself. When he lives theocentrically he realizes himself by reaching out into infinity; he attains his true fulfillment by extending into eternity."[86]

---

[85] Ware, 'Mystery of the Human Person', *Sobornost* 3.1, 1981, p. 69.
[86] P. Nellas, *Deification in Christ*, p. 42.

Eternity—not death—is natural to us. Without this theological and eternal dimension, we fail to be truly human.[87]

We must struggle to attain the fullness of human personhood, within the therapeutic life of Christ's Holy Body—His Holy Church. The Church gives life and sanctifies life. And we too, as Orthodox Christians, must seek to save life and sanctify life—starting with our *own* life, our heart, our mind—our own body.

As Elder Vasileios writes, "Deification is shown to be the process of becoming human."[88]

Every human person, created in the image of Christ, is unique and unrepeatable. We must strive to see the eternal worth of everyone—every single soul—no matter how difficult the character, extent of personal failings, or depth of spiritual flaws: "Perfect love presupposes that you love all men equally."[89]

We close with words of St. Gregory the Theologian, "Let us become like Christ, since Christ also became like us. Let us become gods because of Him, since He also because of us, became human."[90]

---

[87] "Those who are saved—the saints—receive Divine eternity as their [inalienable] possession ..." *Saint Silouan the Athonite,* p. 190.

[88] Archim. Vasileios, *From the Old Adam to the New,* trans. E. Theokritoff, Montreal, 2008, p. 15.

[89] St. Maximos the Confessor, *Texts on Love* 2. 10, PG 90, 988A, trans. *The Philokalia* 2, p. 66.

[90] St. Gregory the Theologian, *Orations* 1. 5, trans. N. Harrison, Crestwood, 2008, p. 59.

Select Bibliography

Patristic Writings

ST. BASIL THE GREAT

———— *Homily Against Those Who Are Prone to Anger.* Trans. N. Harrison. *On the Human Condition.* Crestwood: St. Vladimir's Seminary Press, 2005.

———— *Homily Explaining That God Is Not the Cause of Evil.* Trans. N. Harrison. *On the Human Condition.* Crestwood: St. Vladimir's Seminary Press, 2005.

———— *The Long Rules.* Trans. M. Wagner. The Fathers of the Church. Washington, DC: The Catholic University of America Press, 1962.

ST. GREGORY THE THEOLOGIAN

———— *Festal Orations.* Trans. N. Harrison. Crestwood: St. Vladimir's Seminary Press, 2008.

———— *Select Orations.* Trans. Browne and Swallow. The Nicene and Post-Nicene Fathers, vol. 7. Peabody: Hendrickson Publishers, 2004.

ST. GREGORY OF NYSSA

———— *On the Making of Man.* Trans. H. Wilson. The Nicene and Post-Nicene Fathers, vol. 5. Peabody: Hendrickson Publishers, 2004.

———— *On the Soul and Resurrection.* Trans. C. Roth. Crestwood: St. Vladimir's Seminary Press, 1993.

———— *The Life of Moses.* Trans. Malherbe and Ferguson. Classics of Western Spirituality. New York: Paulist Press, 1978.

ST. GREGORY PALAMAS

———— *The Homilies.* Ed. and Trans. C. Veniamin, Waymart: Mount Thabor Publishing, 2009.

———— *The Natural Chapters.* Trans. Palmer, Sherrard and Ware. The Philokalia, vol. 4. London: Faber and Faber, 1995.

ST. IRENAEUS OF LYON

———— *Against the Heresies.* Trans. Roberts and Donaldson. The Ante-Nicene Fathers, vol. 1. Peabody: Hendrickson Publishers, 2004.

————*On the Apostolic Preaching.* Trans. J. Behr. Crestwood: St. Vladimir's Seminary Press, 1997.

ST. ISAAC THE SYRIAN

———— *The Ascetical Homilies*. Trans. Holy Transfiguration Monastery. Boston: Holy Transfiguration Monastery, 2011.

ST. JOHN CHRYSOSTOM

———— *Homilies on First Corinthians*. Trans. T. Chambers. The Nicene and Post-Nicene Fathers, vol. 12. Peabody: Hendrickson Publishers, 2004.

———— *Homilies on the Psalms*. Trans. R. Hill. Brookline: Holy Cross Press, 2003.

ST. JOHN CLIMACUS

———— *The Ladder of Divine Ascent*. Trans. Luibheid and Russell. Classics of Western Spirituality. New York: Paulist Press, 1982.

ST. JOHN DAMASCENE

———— *Exact Exposition of the Orthodox Faith*. Trans. F. Chase. The Fathers of the Church. Washington, DC: The Catholic University of America Press, 1958.

———— *On the Divine Images*. Trans. D. Anderson. Crestwood: St. Vladimir's Seminary Press, 1980.

St. Macarios of Egypt

———— *The Fifty Spiritual Homilies.* Trans. G. Maloney. Classics of Western Spirituality. New York: Paulist Press, 1992.

St. Mark the Ascetic

———— *On Those Who Think That They are Made Righteous by Works.* Trans. Palmer, Sherrard and Ware. The Philokalia, vol. 1. London: Faber and Faber, 1979.

St. Maximos the Confessor

———— *Four Hundred Texts on Love.* Trans. Palmer, Sherrard and Ware. The Philokalia, vol. 2. London: Faber and Faber, 1981.

———— *On Difficulties in Sacred Scripture: The Responses to Thalassios.* Trans. M. Constas. The Fathers of the Church. Washington, DC: Catholic University of America Press, 2018.

———— *Two Hundred Texts on Theology.* Trans. Palmer, Sherrard and Ware. The Philokalia, vol. 2. London: Faber and Faber, 1981.

———— *Various Texts on Theology.* Trans. Palmer, Sherrard and Ware. The Philokalia, vol. 2. London: Faber and Faber, 1981.

ST. NICHOLAS CABASILAS

———— *Commentary on the Divine Liturgy*. Trans. Hussey and McNulty. Crestwood: St. Vladimir's Seminary Press, 1977.

———— *Homily on the Annunciation*. *Orthodox Tradition* vol. 22. 2. Etna: St. Gregory Palamas Monastery, 2005.

———— *The Life in Christ*. Trans. C. DeCatanzaro. Crestwood: St. Vladimir's Seminary Press, 1974.

Modern Authors

BOOSALIS, Harry. *Knowledge of God.* South Canaan: St. Tikhon's Seminary Press, 2009.

———— *Orthodox Spiritual Life.* South Canaan: St. Tikhon's Seminary Press, 2000.

———— *The Joy of the Holy.* South Canaan: St. Tikhon's Seminary Press, 1993.

FLOROVSKY, Georges. *Creation and Redemption.* Belmont: Nordland Publishing, 1976.

HIEROTHEOS (Vlachos), Metropolitan. *Life After Death.* Trans. E. Williams. Levadia: Birth of the Theotokos Monastery, 1996.

———— *Orthodox Psychotherapy.* Trans. E. Williams. Levadia: Birth of the Theotokos Monastery, 1994.

———— *The Illness and Cure of the Soul in the Orthodox Tradition.* Trans. E. Mavromichali. Levadia: Birth of the Theotokos Monastery, 1993.

———— *The Person in the Orthodox Tradition.* Trans. E. Williams. Levadia: Birth of the Theotokos Monastery, 1999.

JUSTIN (Popovich), Saint. *Faith and Life in Christ*. Trans. A. Gerostergios. Belmont: Institute for Byzantine and Modern Greek Studies, 1994.

———— *Man and the God-man*, Alhambra: St. Sebastian Orthodox Press, 2009.

KESELOPOULOS, Anestis. *Passions and Virtues*. Trans. Hieromonk Alexios (Trader) and H. Boosalis. South Canaan: St. Tikhon's Seminary Press, 2004.

LARCHET, Jean-Claude. *Therapy of Spiritual Illnesses*, vols. 1-3. Trans. K. Sprecher. Montreal: Alexander Press, 2012.

LOSSKY, Vladimir. *In the Image and Likeness of God*. Crestwood: St. Vladimir's Seminary Press, 1985.

———— *The Mystical Theology of the Eastern Church*. Crestwood: St. Vladimir's Seminary Press, 1976.

MANTZARIDIS, Georgios. *Orthodox Spiritual Life*. Trans. K. Schram. Brookline: Holy Cross Press, 1994.

———— *The Deification of Man*. Trans. L. Sherrard. Crestwood: St. Vladimir's Seminary Press, 1984.

———— *Time and Man*. Trans. J. Vulliamy. South Canaan: St. Tikhon's Seminary Press, 1996.

NELLAS, Panayiotis. *Deification in Christ*. Trans. N. Russell. Crestwood: St. Vladimir's Seminary Press, 1987.

PAISIOS, Saint. *Passions and Virtues*. Trans. P. Chamberas. Thessalonica: Holy Monastery of St. John the Evangelist and Theologian, 2016.

———— *Spiritual Struggle*. Trans. P. Chamberas. Thessalonica: Holy Monastery of St. John the Evangelist and Theologian, 2010.

POMAZANSKY, Michael. *Orthodox Dogmatic Theology*. Trans. S. Rose. Platina: St. Herman of Alaska Brotherhood, 2009.

PORPHYRIOS, Saint. *Wounded by Love*. Trans. J. Raffan. Evia: Denise Harvey, 2005.

ROMANIDES, John. *Ancestral Sin*. Trans. G. Gabriel. Ridgewood: Zephyr Publishing, 2002.

SOPHRONY, Archimandrite. *Saint Silouan the Athonite*. Trans. R. Edmonds. Essex: Stavropegic Monastery of St. John the Baptist, 1991.

———— *We Shall See Him as He Is*. Trans. R. Edmonds. Essex: Stavropegic Monastery of St. John the Baptist, 1988.

STANILOAE, Dumitru. *The Experience of God*, vols. 1-2. Trans. Ionita and Barringer. Brookline: Holy Cross Press, 1994 and 2000.

THADDEUS, Elder. *Our Thoughts Determine Our Lives*, trans. A. Smiljanic, Platina: St. Herman of Alaska Brotherhood, 2010.

THEOKRITOFF, Elizabeth. *Living In God's Creation*. Crestwood: St. Vladimir's Seminary Press, 2009.

VASILEIOS, Archimandrite. *From the Old Adam to the New*. Trans. E. Theokritoff. Montreal: Alexander Press, 2008.

—— *Hymn of Entry*. Trans. E. Brière (Theokritoff). Crestwood: St. Vladimir's Seminary Press, 1984.

—— *The Divine Liturgy as a Theophany of the Holy Trinity*. Trans. E. Theokritoff. Montreal: Alexander Press, 2015.

—— *The Saint: Archetype of Orthodoxy*. Trans. E. Theokritoff. Montreal: Alexander Press, 1997.

ZACHARIAS, Archimandrite. *Remember Thy First Love*. Ed. C. Veniamin. Waymart: Mount Thabor Publishing, 2016.